THE DEFIANT WOMAN

FIGHTING IN THE FRENCH RESISTANCE

FRANÇOISE PÈNE

Why aren't we born old? We would know to act wisely on the slow journey to our carefree and joyful youth. Death would claim us in the ignorant bliss of infancy.

Françoise Pène

THE DEFIANT WOMAN

FIGHTING IN THE
FRENCH RESISTANCE

Françoise Pène

Translated from the French original
by Janet E. Martin

Leonard Press
Bolivar, Missouri
2018

Originally published as *Françoise Pène: La vie d'une femme résistante* by Éditions Grandvaux, ©2013 ISBN 978-2909550862.

Cover design by Samuel Trobisch

Cover photography from the private photo collection belonging to the Pène family. Unless otherwise indicated, all photographs originate from the private photo collection of the Pène family.

ISBN 9781931475679
Library of Congress Control Number: 2018933710

We wish to thank Éditions Grandvaux,
publisher of the original French edition of
Françoise Pène: La vie d'une femme résistante,
2013, for making available the rights for the
English translation.

TRANSLATOR'S NOTE

I feel very privileged to have come to know the Pène family through my role as translator of their mother's incredible memoir. It is my great hope that I have captured in English the life she lived so well, with courage and resourcefulness, through exciting and dangerous times.

Janet E. Martin

FOREWORD

This is the memoir of Françoise Pène, née Françoise Lévy-Neumand in 1904. Hers was a life worthy of a novel! In 1925, she married Pierre Pène and the young couple was thrust as witnesses of, and active participants in the dawning era of turbulent 20th century history. She died in 1997, her life having spanned almost the entire century.

Hers was an extraordinary life and her memoir is a vivid and historic tale, fascinating and exciting, a "page turner". Françoise wrote the bulk of her memoir in the 1960s and it was polished and edited twenty years later. Her family decided to publish it now because we are at a watershed moment: the last remaining witnesses to this story, Françoise's children, are still among us. It is important that *their* descendants inherit this story. They and others of their generation must keep the memory so as to benefit from the courage and fortitude in these pages and take from them inspiration to confront the problems of the world today. This book must serve as a dialogue between the generations. After risking their lives and surviving World War II, Françoise and

Pierre had 31 descendants, 30 still alive today.

Born in Epernay in France's Champagne region, Françoise witnessed the deployment of troops and the trenches of WWI from the "Montagne de Reims" nearby. She recounts the air raid alerts, enemy planes and war news, marking the first tragedy of her life. Her father died when she was almost eleven years old. He had been poisoned by gas warfare of WWI. The family flees to the refuge of Grenoble where she attends school and studies decorative arts, culminating in a career as a painter. It is there that she encounters Pierre Pène, a meeting that will seal her fate. A graduate of the prestigious Ecole Polytechnique, Pierre is a bridge and tunnel engineer and, like many of the young people of his generation, is sent to serve abroad in France's colonies.

And so we dive into the life of the young couple as they discover Madagascar and its people. Françoise shares her feelings as a young wife and new mother to their first child, a daughter. Their adventures continue to Ethiopia, then the only independent African nation, where they attend the coronation of its Emperor. They discover the rich culture of Addis Ababa of the 1930s with its thousand year old history, its traditions and its haughty pride. We journey with their caravan through the Omo Valley, rich in archeology and exotic wildlife, to the pomp and ostentation of Emperor Haile Selassie's court. There, Françoise has a brush with death when, suffering from the effects of altitude, she gives birth to a second daughter.

In 1933, they return to the joys of Paris, the friends and the dancing they so loved. A son is born. Pierre is assigned to the quiet town of Soissons but threats to world's peace are brewing. Pierre is called to military service. The disaster of France's defeat and occupation causes Françoise to flee for the second time, this time to Pierre's ancestral home in the Pyrénées.

Françoise and Pierre are in agreement: the fight must go on.

Pierre joins the Resistance. Bridge engineers enjoy a certain freedom of movement with attendant benefits in intelligence gathering. In 1942 and 1943, the Resistance begins to take military action, initiate sabotage attacks and shelter and repatriate downed allied airmen. Pierre joins the Organization Civile et Militaire (OCM) , a branch of the Resistance, as head for the regions of Aisne and Ardennes. At the end of 1943 he becomes head of the Forces Françaises de l'Interieur (FFI) for Paris region. Pierre was succeeded in that role by his colleague Rol Tanguy when he was arrested on April 4, 1944. Pierre was tortured but escaped and lived clandestinely in Paris, changing safe houses daily at great peril to him and to those who risked their lives to save him.

Another son is born and soon thereafter, Françoise is arrested and interrogated. But she avoids the traps of the interrogation, denying any and all involvement in the Resistance: we are witness to her verbal duel with her wily and clever interrogator. As a Jew, she faces the worst possible consequences, but she fights like a cornered lioness with cubs. She suffers another brush with death in the solitary confinement of Fresnes prison where she is held.

Her elder children, left to themselves, take Françoise's place in the clandestine activities aiding their father. Resistance meant also treason; Pierre lived it as related by Françoise. Pursued as terrorists, they would all, parents and children, make it through alive.

In August of 1944, Paris is liberated and Pierre, named "Commissaire de la République" at St. Quentin, has to cross German lines again, as head of the FFI, to lead the liberation of the four departments he is to administer. Françoise meanwhile cares for prisoners returning from the German camps. De Gaulle leaves power and the "Commissaires de la République" are disbanded. Pierre is named Governor of Germany's Bade region. An engineer by training and a Resistance fighter by necessity, he now takes on the role of high level administrator, assisting with

Germany's reconstruction and playing an important role in Germany's reconciliation with France, as well as in the genesis of the European Union whose founder, Robert Schuman, was a frequent visitor to Pierre and Françoise's home.

Meanwhile, Françoise has traded the dungeon for a "château" at Umkirch, where she reigns, creating a stable life for Pierre and their family and serving as hostess to the famous people of the day.

Dare we say that Pierre was a hero, he and those like him who joined the Resistance out of conviction? They were outraged and they took action. The "career path" of the Resistance was torture and death, and so many died this way! Postwar, those who survived found themselves thrust into the highest levels of responsibility, ill prepared, perhaps, but totally committed to a goal greater than their personal ambitions, committed to their cause. They weren't saints. They all had their human frailties, but courage and faith in their values sustained them even in the face of martyrdom.

With Germany coming back to life, the family returns to France no better off than they had left due to Pierre's scrupulous honesty. A new assignment sends Pierre to Monaco as the Prince's Consultant for Public Works and the family delves into a new life there.

As soon as she was able, Françoise resumed painting and still today we admire the many beautiful and moving works she produced. She speaks of life's pain and suffering, of Pierre's death and the anticipation of her own. She confronts it all with the same courage with which she faced her German interrogator.

Her lesson deserves a book.

Olivier de Fresnoye and Olivier Pène

Contents

FOREWORD i

CONTENTS..v

PREFACE vii

CHAPTER ONE
My Youth 9

CHAPTER TWO
Madagascar...21

CHAPTER THREE
Ethiopia – The Omo Valley 29

CHAPTER FOUR
The Phony War 1939-1940..49

CHAPTER FIVE
The Early Years of the Resistance 55

CHAPTER SIX
Françoise in the Nazi Dungeon 69

CHAPTER SEVEN
Pierre, "Commissaire de la République"..85

CHAPTER EIGHT
Pierre – Governor of the German State of Baden 91

CHAPTER NINE
In Service of the Prince of Monaco...121

CHAPTER TEN
Taking up Painting again...135

CHAPTER ELEVEN
The Final Years 153

Françoise at 18 with her friends in Grenoble

Françoise and Pierre 1925

PREFACE

Have I had a fulfilled life and how will I finish it? It's not death that bothers me. On the contrary, death holds for me a long rest and the end of pondering thoughts with no answers. It wouldn't be bearable to live indefinitely. However the idea of physical and mental decay bothers me a little more each day.

As a young girl, I wanted to be a stained glass artist so, after high school, I enrolled in a decorative arts school to apprentice in this beautiful craft. My goal was to replace the stained glass windows destroyed in WWI and achieve the level of craftsmanship of the old masters. I didn't want to copy them but, rather, to use their instinctive harmony to inspire me to something new. But meeting my soulmate and raising my family changed my plans. The budding artist gave way to a woman of the world, focused on her husband's career and the joys of motherhood.

Later, when we returned from our travels in Africa, looking at the works of Rouault and Chagall, I realized that these masters had achieved my dreams. I picked up the paintbrush at different times of my life without ever really getting a fix on the value of my canvases or identifying myself with a particular trend or school of painting. I always tried to paint expressing my temperament, impulses, imagination, not conforming to trends.

Even if, since I have done exhibitions, I consider myself a

professional painter, my fame never extended beyond a certain circle. I'll never know if that was a blessing. All the same, my application for professional status with the appropriate credentials was approved on October 1, 1949, by Paul Landowski (the famous sculptor who carved the statue of Christ which graces Rio de Janeiro).

Born Jewish, I converted to Catholicism to please my mother-in-law who wanted her grandchildren baptized, but also because my mother, a war widow free to make her own choices, had always steered her children, through artistic education, toward Catholicism which inspired so many masterpieces. After Nazism and its atrocities, my feelings changed and I have since schooled myself in Judaism and have never ceased to be interested in the state of Israel.

Pierre has been gone for twenty years despite the fact that we always wanted to die at the same time; we spoke about that often to the point that it became a comforting thought. The idea of being separated after nearly fifty years together seemed unbearable. But fate decided otherwise.

We leave four children, eight grandchildren and fourteen great grandchildren, so we never really die completely.

This book is the living proof.

Françoise Pène

ONE

My Youth

Grenoble, November 1924. Night had fallen on the town and the smell of wood fire smoke perfumed its streets... Arms linked, we hurried along, Toino and I, to a get-together with friends.

It was the third surprise party of the week and it would be an evening of dancing. Tango, fox-trot, waltz, and other slow dances ... in this postwar period, all the rhythms lent themselves to having fun and looking at the bright side of life. I even managed to rise to a challenge: dance beyond midnight for a fortnight straight without developing circles under my eyes!

Always in the know, our friend Robert alerted us to "the arrival of two new dance participants, intelligent guys, graduates of the Ecole Polytechnique". As we learned their names, Toino announced "I pick Marc Henry" and I, "Pierre Pène". Premonition or chance of fate, these two young men would become, seven months later, our respective husbands!

But let's get back to that first encounter. Introductions were dispensed with quickly and I was immediately impressed by my new suitor. Tall, dark and handsome, Pierre Pène, a roads and bridges engineer, had large eyes that sparkled with humor and a droll smile. He had broad shoulders but a lean physique.

When he took me in his arms for our first dance, a slow number, I noticed right away what a fine dancer he was. Our bodies fit together perfectly. A little shorter than he and a little more curvy than the "boyish" trend of the day, with my blond curls, light complexion, grey/green eyes and a taunting smile, I was pretty. And I never lacked suitors inviting me out.

That was, by the way, the subject of our first falling out.

"My Lord, it's 2 a.m. and I have to inaugurate a new tram line at dawn" Pierre exclaimed, leaning toward me as he made his move to leave.

"No matter" said I, feigning an air of indifference even as he obviously expected me to go home as well. "I have other dance partners".

Angry at my flirtatious attitude, Pierre uttered not another word to me and turned on his heel. I had no idea how sensitive he was! Worse, during the ensuing weeks, he made it his business to dance under my nose with one of my friends, older and quite ugly and very eager to avoid becoming an old maid!

We made up over a very strong brandy alexander, handed out by a strange American guy at the door to a wild party. After a few minutes of lively discussion, seated on a couch in soft, dim lighting, we mocked couples who were making out, rare in those days, when young women who allowed themselves to be kissed risked developing a reputation. Pierre kissed me on the eyelids. By the end of the evening we were walking on air.

In the ensuing weeks, with each passing day, Pierre became more and more present in my life, frequently visiting my home under the pretext of consulting our art books. He later confessed that, when we had first met, he had promised himself not to fall in love with me ...

Wanting to continue to pursue my studies at the School of Decorative Arts in Grenoble, where we had taken refuge during

WWI, I too wanted to remain single. But Pierre's charm, sense of humor and intelligence got the better of me.

As always in such situations, my mother knew what was developing long before I did. Considering me too young, she tried to discourage me from letting this budding romance go any further but she eventually embraced our getting married.

As a fatherless minor, I had to get permission from my uncle and guardian, Dr. Neumand. His medical practice was in Salins and Marnoz in the Jura region. In the only instance, since my father's death, of him executing his duty as guardian, he let me know with a few words written on the back of a prescription script "You can marry if I approve of him"; to which I replied "If you refuse, I will wait until I am of legal age". When my uncle learned of Pierre's professional career prospects, he finally approved, again with a terse note, "I am delighted with your choice of fiancé".

Thus our marriage took place without further delay, Pierre at 27 and I at 20 years of age. It was the beginning of a long life together, full of adventures, happiness and success; my childhood seemed already a fleeting memory.

I was born in Epernay in 1904 to Jewish parents originally from Alsace. They left Alsace Lorraine following the Prussian War.

My mother was crazy about a Catholic architect and poet but, pressured by her father, settled for an arranged marriage. It was a lost cause from the start. All she wanted was to live the life of a Parisian, musician, and art lover, surrounded by her parents and five brothers and a sister in Paris or at the beach. My father retaliated by having affairs with the hired help.

I loved my sweet, beautiful mother who gave us a great deal of freedom which we did not abuse. She was not interested in who said what to whom. She was devoted to culture, preferring philosophers to novelists, classical music to operettas. Literally captivated by the piano, she did not allow herself to be distracted by mundane tasks such as cooking and cleaning. Thus it was to the maid that we presented our requests when my sister, brother and I wanted a favorite dish.

By contrast, my father was always busy and stressed and paid little attention to us. He was a banker but had suffered setbacks from bad investments. Then he had inherited a prosperous grain business from his father but shut it down during WWI following a long illness that had prompted his discharge from the military and eventually caused his death.

My sister Elisabeth and I, having very different personalities, got along famously. On the other hand, I never much cared for my brother Alain. Always coddled by my mother and sister on the grounds that he was fragile, he racked up no small amount of misdeeds reflecting his jealous, tattle-tale and angry nature.

When I was young, I told my mother constantly that her spoiling him would have dire consequences but she wouldn't listen and it cost her dearly. He married too young and proved incapable of supporting his wife and children; his wife abandoned him.

Zabeth, as I called Elisabeth, was the best girl in the world, full of common sense, low key, always late and given to bursts of anger or laughter, as unexpected as they were intense. Brunette with a mane of unruly hair, she blossomed suddenly at puberty. While my blond curls and fair complexion elicited constant and unwelcome compliments, I was a tomboy. My greatest pleasure was perching myself high in a tree with a book, exactly where my mother would have difficulty finding me for our mandatory daily three-hour piano practice, one of several obligations we couldn't avoid.

I also remember cold showers every morning except the two days a week when we would bathe. Also, the daily walk we'd make to the same place. Whatever the weather, we would climb the side of the St. Laurent mountain to the dried up waterfall overlooking the Marne Valley. The, in my opinion, monotonous and boring outings allowed my mother to determine the proximity of enemy attacks and the intensity of the cannon fire. We were right on the front line of WWI.

Epernay's location in the east of France, close to the front on the other side of the "Montagne de Reims", had attracted the French general staff, (as had the champagne cellars), which led the German Tauben plane squads to bomb the town. My sister and I liked to watch from the garden of my grandmother's house above the town where we would stay for 4 or 5 days each month when clear skies and full moon favored attacks. A defensive position set up at a spot known as "La Cascade" (the waterfall), tried during alerts to thwart the attack by blinding the pilots, spotting the planes and strafing them with gun fire. This odd fireworks display always fascinated Zab and me, outside in the garden in our nightgowns.

One night we even saw, by the light of a large flare, a plane come in very low, with all the danger that implies, to deposit via a rope a man onto the mountain. By chance, my mother went the next day to the town to attend a burial in a spot just next to that of the drop off. During the early morning funeral, the service was distracted by a man attempting to conceal himself; the obsession with wartime espionage had begun. The man was turned over to the army and executed the same day.

When the sirens went off during the school day, we hurried down to the shelter of the magnificent champagne cellars of Moët et Chandon! It was a very pleasant ritual. After quickly grabbing our wool sweaters from the backs of our chairs, a gas mask and an emergency supply of almonds, raisins and dried figs, we assembled by grade to go down a huge staircase leading to the school's cellar which connected to that of Moët et Chandon. The teachers followed and our school director, like a captain at the helm of her ship, awaited the last one before beginning her own slow and majestic descent to join us.

No sooner than we reached the bottom of the stairs we would launch into games of hide and seek and circle dances. We also chatted with the workers employed to turn the precious bottles of champagne. One day, in twirling around a bit too fast, we broke a jeroboam (which holds the equivalent of four bottles) of the developing nectar. Our head mistress was furious.

As the bombings would most often take place at night, the teachers would camp at the best shelter, namely the school. Then during the day, these ladies who had held vigil and chatted into the wee hours would tell us to put our heads on our desks and nap. One morning when we had been prohibited from going to school because of a prior attack, I decided to go with my sister to the train station about which the adults were constantly talking with concern. The sight of the wounded and dead, some burned, will be fixed in my memory forever.

By contrast to my mother, my grandmother was a perfect homemaker. At her house, the meals were always marvelous, homemade dishes (with the help of a cook) such as smoked tongue, choucroute (a dish of sauerkraut, meats and sausages) and all sorts of desserts. Every Friday, we would go directly from school to pay a visit to her and my grandfather at their huge home with a large and beautifully maintained yard, including to be sure, a vegetable garden and a chicken coop.

Our own garden was wild but we rather liked it. We could excavate trenches and play war games with the neighborhood kids. We even built a "cagna" in the trenches to cook potatoes in the embers. Only the kids playing the "French" forces got the best shelter with curtains of long green growth. The "German" forces had to settle for trenches dug among the potato plants.

I also have a wonderful memory of the time when I was 13 and we went to spend several days with our maid Pauline and her 12 brothers and sisters in Boursault to do the grape harvest for her parents. The vintners all helped each other during the harvest and we would go from vineyard to vineyard to work. Up at dawn, we would start with a cup of coffee – an exciting drink I never had at home – at the home of the wine grower for whom we were working that day. By 5 a.m. we were working in the vines with our snack of bread, lard and nuts. Each person chose a row and, armed with scissors and a basket, would begin cutting the heavy purple bunches. Taking my work seriously, I tried to get to the end of my row at the same time as the vineyard workers. That didn't prohibit me from tasting as many of the grapes as I wanted. In the evening, the harvesters would gather again at the farmhouse where a large table was set up on the lawn. A veritable feast would ensue with traditional cabbage and bacon soup, sausages, stuffed roasted chicken or rabbit with peas, local cheeses and huge fruit tarts.

After dinner, we all went to the wine-press where the juice from the grapes was already bubbling in the vats. We tasted the nectar and put long ladles into the vats to refill our glasses before heading to bed as very happy angels ... until morning came and we were pulled sleepily out of bed.

My childhood sailed along, punctuated by celebrations, games and reading. I especially remember long stretches in the attic in the spot reserved for fruit drying racks, with Zabeth, poring over photo albums of the great exhibitions of the 19th century or "La Petite Illustration" which published all the new plays. Articles about the Dreyfus Affair abounded (a scandal involving the wrongful conviction and imprisonment of a Jewish Alsatian military officer) and we looked at the political cartoons it generated without really comprehending much. At my paternal grandparents' home, we found books such as novels by Dickens, Uncle Tom's Cabin, as well as full collections of contemporary theater, Labiche, Courteline, etc.

Mom took us regularly to the library and took great care to oversee what we were reading. She was particularly pleased with my passion for world literature.

But she didn't show any concern for our religious education. My classmates, the majority of whom were Catholic, were little different from us, except, around 12 years of age, when they were preparing for their First Holy Communion. Some of them would occasionally say hurtful things without our understanding the reason. It was because the catechism they studied repeatedly said the Jews killed Christ. Poor us. What could we do?

And who could imagine that these barbs would be the prelude to the biggest genocide the world had ever seen with the passive acceptance of a huge number of good people?

Our lives barely changed when my father died. He hadn't ever bothered much with us and showed little affection. Sure, our standard of living suffered a little, but mom had enough that she did not need to work. She adapted well to tightening her belt and played the piano for hours every day and even invited a young blind man from Rheims to enjoy the delights of music. She learned braille so as to transcribe piano scores for him. He thus became my piano teacher without showing more zeal than his student for his task. He was like a big brother to the family until 1918 when we headed for the seaside town of La Baule in Brittany following a brief stay in Paris. It was in Paris that we became acquainted with the capabilities of "Big Bertha", a long range cannon installed by the Germans about 100 kilometers away. We joined my grandparents in La Baule, along with several Parisian cousins.

New life, new pleasures ... Despite the heavy mood of war, which cast a dark cloud whenever the adults would come back from the train station where war news was posted, the four months at the Atlantic seaside was a great adventure of swimming, shell collecting, sand castles, and meals in nearby Pornichet or Pouliguen.

For Zab and me it was also a time of quarantine and fasting due to an illness with unusual symptoms. We had caught the infamous Spanish influenza which we were later told had claimed more victims than WWI! My grandfather attached tags to our bowls so they wouldn't be confused with the others, shook out the cushions to get rid of any microbes (from which point we could no longer use them) and other precautions to successfully protect the rest of the household.

At that time, mom explored the Dauphiné area, rediscovering the beautiful mountains she had liked so well when on vacation in Uriage when she was 18 and fell in love with a Catholic architect her father would not allow her to marry. Immediately charmed by Grenoble, fleeing the final German advance, she found us a new place to live and we joined her there in September. We settled in immediately. Mom, who had a magnificent voice, joined the professional choir of the Berlioz orchestra.

She also forged a relationship with the conservator of the local museum, a short, rotund, dynamic man, passionate about modern art, who gave me my first painting lessons. He was Pierre André-Farcy, the noted poster painter and art critic who opened his own contemporary art museum and developed an international following.

His gift of gab delighted my mother and me. He refused to be paid for my lessons, saying he was too expensive for a war widow, and would instead advise us on a friendly basis. He trained me more as a critic than as a painter, always telling me "Don't get caught up in the details, look for the essence of the work".

I can still see him looking through my mother's library as she read her literary and artistic reviews. He would seek her advice on how to exhibit his acquisitions, very happy to show his new treasures, his contemporary artist canvases, and recent avant-garde selections from Paris where he often went.

I felt equally comfortable at school in Grenoble. There were so few Jews in this large, dynamic city that one didn't perceive the anti-Semitism of the east where so many Alsatians had settled in order to remain French following the Franco Prussian War in 1870. I also loved our apartment, warm and cozy with its pink oven made of Alsatian pottery, its old furniture, large red easy chairs – worn but comfortable – in which I often found myself.

And when being with mom, beautiful Helene, life was good, focused on looking outward, open to culture, to music and to numerous friends they brought with them. They included the quartet of professional musicians who came to play with the talented pianist she was, as well as students who lingered after lessons, never in a hurry to leave. One of them, met at a university conference on the topic of Pascal, was a big guy from Rheims who had returned from the war that killed all of his friends; some years later, he would become my brother-in-law.

My only annoyance of youth was failing to get my high school diploma. The rigor of the exam was underestimated in the girls' schools which focused too much and too long on the difference between the sexes. Only female students pursuing studies in pharmacy or medicine were authorized to take the test for the diploma, known as "le bac", short for baccalaureate. Our school director, mean and old fashioned, wanted at any price to uphold the value of this venerable old test, and she set the bar very high. Despite my reputation as a good and conscientious student, I was weak in foreign languages and math, and I failed German, which was no doubt a fair assessment, disqualifying me. Although frustrated by this setback, I had no need of the bac to enter the School of Decorative Arts in Grenoble.

I don't regret my choice because I liked art school, including plasterwork and industrial design. I did extremely well in fabric, wallpaper, bookbinding and stained glass etc., in which I had a prodigious production that surprised my colleagues for its audacity and nature.

Our professor, Mr. Burkalter, a young man with a mild limp,

was adored by all the students. Thanks to him, our work was a joy. Influenced by the Cubists and their friends Le Corbusier, Mallet-Stevens, and the Martel brothers, he oriented us toward the same spirit of simplification which contrasted with the heavy, overwrought decoration of 19th century works.

But we wanted to innovate and find a style all our own. Each semester, I got into the next class but then, Mr. Burkalter quit because of a dispute with the school's director during which he called the director pompous. That left me and my three closest friends in the lurch, but we carried on.

The oldest and least attractive of our group, Germaine, was determined to find a husband before she became an old maid. She met and married a nice guy, younger than she, who worked in the manufacture of toilet paper. They moved to the countryside, near the factory, and had a lovely little girl.

The most elegant one, Yvonne, daughter of the departmental "préfet" and used to evenings on the town, would seek out admirers and flirt platonically from a distance. That didn't keep her from falling for a guy who was in love with someone else. Finally she married for money, not love, had a son, was widowed by a car accident, and later took up with one of her old beaux, Toino's brother Guillaume, who abandoned his wife and four children for her.

Daughter of a famous university professor, Raoul Blanchard, Toino was my best friend. She was uproarious and eccentric, prone to gaffes but intelligent, a poor student but very streetwise. It was together that we met the young men who would become our husbands. Thus 1925 marks the end of the quartet of school friends and my adolescence. Germaine married Sombardier in June 1925: Pierre and I in July; Toino and Marc in September. Toino and Marc left for Dakar, Senegal as we were heading for Madagascar. The Sombardiers settled in the suburbs of Grenoble, at Pont-de-Claix, and Yvonne, still single, follows her father to a posting in Marseille.

Françoise and Pierre in Madagascar

Françoise and her daughters in Addis Ababa in 1932

TWO

MADAGASCAR

Comfortably settled in the sunken hollow of our bed, from which we had a view of the road to Brest, I dreamily contemplated the life awaiting me – Pierre, his career, my role as woman of the world, the children to come, my love of painting ... All of a sudden, a head appeared at the top of a ladder against the window. Hastily wrapping myself in the sheet to preserve my modesty, I wondered about this strange intrusion. Workers were affixing a plaque commemorating a writer who previously resided there, Louis Heiman, author of "Maria Chapdelaine", while earnest gentlemen prepared their comments for the dedication.

"Not important" I told myself, deciding to get up anyway. Nothing was going to spoil the honeymoon of a gratified young woman in love.

Pierre had gone out to meet up with his friends from Polytechnique who worked in maritime engineering and would meet me later for a tour on a mahogany powerboat with shimmering copper detailing that he had at his disposal, along with two sailor-pilots. We also planned to see the battleships under construction – the same ones which would be destroyed in

1942, scuttled, serving neither the Allies nor the Germans who had by then invaded the Free Zone.

Later we dined with Pierre's parents and sister whom I had invited to meet us and whom I really liked.

Thin and rather short, my father-in-law very elegantly sported a beard in the style of Napoleon III. My mother-in-law's height did not carry her weight well and she had no sense of style, even wearing homemade hats, but her sense of humor, perfectly matched to her husband's, made up for these shortcomings.

Of country stock, my father-in-law was not able to pursue higher education. He held some modest jobs that were beneath his capabilities, which caused him to be rather withdrawn. Or was it the other way around? After years of working for the Paris-Orléans railroad, putting in many extra hours to support his three children, he fell seriously ill at the age of 42 and retired early at a severely reduced pension. He adored bel canto opera and geography. My mother-in-law was a great gourmand and a fabulous cook. She was also a keen observer of things around her and thus she knew before anyone when I became pregnant.

My sister-in-law, Clotilde, was deeply affected by the death of her older brother, Henri, who succumbed at age 21 following 22 months in the hospital after being horribly wounded in WWI. She sought peace in a very austere life dominated by her studies. I nevertheless managed to nudge her to pick herself up, put on some makeup and cut her hair. She later said she really enjoyed her visit with us.

The days came and went to the rhythm of the tides until we learned, three months after our arrival, that we would be leaving Brest. The ministry in charge of France's colonies had contacted Pierre. We were leaving for Madagascar and it would take the fastest boat of the fleet, the Dombea, at least 28 days to reach the island in the Indian Ocean.

Despite sea sickness and morning sickness, the crossing was delightful and we enjoyed ourselves thoroughly. Orchestras and dancing at teatime and after dinner, deck tennis – where I made the finals, matched against a burly American – masked balls, and a lottery and traditional ceremony to mark for the first timers their crossing of the equator, which included being thrown into a canvas bath. Pierre was horrified to see me, in my pregnant state, tossed in, and tried in vain to protect me from Neptune's clutches. Despite my pregnancy, during that trip I lost 15 pounds that I never gained back.

Pierre's Polytechnique friends were waiting for us at our arrival in Madagascar's capital, Antananarivo; they were kind, mischievous and full of pranks. They gave us quinine, which was essential, as well as Stovarsol, convincing us that it was as easy in Madagascar to catch syphilis as malaria!

These new friends proved to be very nice, if insular, taking turns dining in each other's homes. This got stale pretty fast, so Pierre and I decided to organize dance parties at a converted masonic lodge hall which allowed us to get to know some of the locals and businesspeople.

The house we lived in was modest but pleasant, surrounded by a simple garden of roses and enormous mimosa trees. Nearby, was a huge, three-tiered mausoleum with a small door that led inside so one could visit the dead. Local culture dictated that, every 6 months, relatives of the dead had to change the "lamba" , a colorful handmade fabric that served as a shroud. This practice would eventually be forbidden by the French authorities because it fostered the spread of bubonic plague, as did the long burial ceremonies during which the body would be carted around to numerous stops where family and friends would dance, drink and eat. From our veranda, we watched these picturesque and joyful processions which went on, as a precaution, during the night.

Determined to decorate our house in accordance with my tastes, I hurried to look for inexpensive items at the local market, the "Zouma", and designed several pieces of furniture to be made using the local rosewood; we would thus have a dwelling very different from those of our friends who were content to buy the ubiquitous local rattan model from colleagues who were leaving the island.

Pierre was frequently away on business. He expected to be gone for 8 days but would remain in the bush for 3 weeks. There was a rule against spouses accompanying their husbands on their official expeditions; travel was by sedan chair with each passenger requiring 8 porters. There was no rule against mistresses accompanying them, however, and several took advantage of the loophole. Pierre found what he needed – the gentle "ramatoas", despite their STDs, had their charms.

Throughout these long days, my pregnancy progressed without a problem and Annette, my first daughter, entered the world following a long night, 5 months after our arrival in Madagascar. We couldn't reach the doctor or the midwife. Luckily, the wives of two colleagues came over but worried Pierre who became frightened over a minor medical glitch. Their presence proved critical because, both scrupulously concerned with hygiene, they oversaw the sterilization of the birthing table brought over from the laundry and prevented the maid, Razafy, from using her hands to remove two flies that had fallen into the boiled water.

In 18 years, the doctor, who had married a local woman with whom he had many children, had forgotten Pasteur's principles. He was responsible for numerous puerperal fevers at a time (1926) when antibiotics had not yet been discovered.

Medical help finally arrived a few minutes before Annette's rending and triumphant arrival. She was a normal weight but, once cleaned up, she looked like a tiny porcelain doll. She took center stage in our lives as well as in the letters I sent every fortnight with each boat to my mother and mother-in-law. It would be another 3 years before the first seaplane would make the voyage, lifting off from the lake near Antananarivo, cutting the time to 7 days from the 30 day crossing by boat.

The whites, referred to as "Vazas", and the blacks got along well enough. In spite of a certain reserve, relations were more or less friendly. The natives who worked in the homes of the whites made a better living than their counterparts. They were called "detachable collars" because of the taste they developed for European dress.

Built high above Antananarivo, the wooden hut of Queen Ranavalo III was the distinctive historical remnant marking the revolutionary period; the 1897 rebellion by the indigenous people permitted the Governor General of Madagascar, General Gallieni, to exile the Queen – having held her responsible for the insurrection – crush the rebellion and place the colony under military and political organization.

The town was composed of small hills with red laterite houses the color of the soil. It overlooked terraced rice paddies glistening with water. It was a beautiful town where the women moved gracefully about, draped in their white "lambas".

The bushland had a different kind of charm, more striking and picturesque, which I had a chance to discover during a trip with Pierre that was not work related. What a pleasure to be welcomed into a native hut, to see the canoes piloted by men in red loin-cloths, living in perfect harmony with nature. And what a feeling to have to constantly be on the lookout for the comings and goings of snakes and crocodiles. Pierre was a very good shot and bagged four small crocodiles which ended up making a superb travel bag, as well as several monstrous ones – real man eaters at 20 feet long.

In 1926, there were about 400 victims annually of this horrible beast which, curiously, was deified by the locals, explaining the attitude of the women turning their backs on this mortal danger to do their wash in the river. Less fatalistic, the canoe pilots sang and made noise to keep the enemy at bay.

Following the local rhythm, our lives passed pleasantly. Only Pierre's violent outbursts of temper cast shadows on our relationship, especially when, unable to contain his mood swings, I rebelled against what I perceived as unfairness. Experience led me to try to get him to talk so I could placate him and minimize the importance of the source of his anger – or close myself up in the bathroom until he fell asleep. Unfortunately, at Antananarivo, we had only a small shower room and the door did not lock!

We stayed 4 years in Madagascar because the governor insisted my husband, who was serving as the head of the planning office and adjutant director, smooth the transition of the incoming director of public works. And so it was that I met the only man, other than Pierre, who meant anything in my life. Married and the father of many children born one after the other, this new director, whom I shall not name, made a strong impression on me from our first meeting.

Tall, blond, with a short mustache and large, sweet blue eyes, he was always very calm. Unlike the other colleagues, used to their male privileges, he helped his wife, getting up at night to give bottles to the babies, which made his Polytechnique buddies smirk. When an umpteenth child was expected, it fell to me as a young wife to live with Pierre at their house while his wife was in labor at the hospital. I also had to manage their move as they were leaving that house to take over the official residence of his predecessor.

Pierre's extended absences, totaling almost 12 months in the bush during our 4 year stay, as well as his angry outbursts, pushed me closer to his boss who never cared for long trips away. Naive and outspoken, I warned Pierre of this danger. He took the threat too seriously. I tried to backpedal, to minimize the importance of the relationship which was, after all, platonic. But Pierre, on alert because of my stupid admission, caught us alone one day. He thought we were kissing and reacted violently, striking his colleague who took it without a word. A few days later, his wife, who evidently found out somehow, was very nasty toward me.

Luckily our departure date approached. Despite the pain of the separation, Mr. X and I agreed it was for the best.

Pierre and I were supposed to return to Madagascar, known as the pink island, following an 8 month hiatus in France, but a chance meeting aboard ship with a Mr. La Rivière led us instead to Ethiopia.

The return voyage to France included a stop in Suez which gave us the chance to take a train to Cairo to see the Sphinx, the Pyramids, and the treasure of Tutankhamen's tomb which was discovered in 1922 and was on display at the Cairo Museum.

Was it because of the climate, Pierre's bouts of anger or the unpleasantness of the Mr. X mini-drama that, upon arrival in France I felt physically very weak? It was bad but did not prevent us from going out dancing often.

We stayed in Montmartre during our visit to Paris, taking over a pleasant studio my brother had above the Rue du Mont-Cenis. Pierre wasn't working and was no longer angry at his innocent wife. The grandparents were taking turns caring for Annette, a cute but headstrong little girl. Neither my mother-in-law's strictness nor my mother's permissiveness worked in managing her. We undeserving parents used our freedom to take in shows and go to dances, sometimes masked balls. Prior to returning to the tropics, we spent our money liberally and didn't worry about saving.

Meanwhile, the medical diagnosis of my fatigue proved to be tuberculosis forcing us to forsake Paris and its dances and theater for Pierre's hometown village, Cier-de-Rivière in the Pyrenees. There we lived a healthy and calm existence which allowed us to be ready to depart for Ethiopia in November of 1930.

The first page of our life had turned.

Pierre in Ethiopia in 1932

Françoise and Pierre in 1936

THREE

ETHIOPIA—
THE OMO VALLEY

Always excited at the prospect of discovering a new country, we were to arrive in Ethiopia two months prior to the coronation of the "King of Kings", Haile Selassie. After a twelve day crossing on the ship from Marseille to Djibouti, we boarded the Franco-Ethiopian train which would take another three days to reach the capital, Addis Ababa. The train stopped at noon and in the evening and we took our meals in the desert in small inns run by Greeks or Armenians.

The stop at Diredawa, a town with a temperate climate, developed during the difficult and deadly construction of the rail line, was particularly pleasant. At dawn the next day, we resumed our journey. The countryside rolled by, mostly wild and barren, but resplendent with colorful birds.

When nightfall approached, the train stopped for safety reasons. The locals frequently removed sections of rail to make spears, and herds of wild beasts would cross the tracks.

As at Antananarivo, the comradery of the Polytechnicians was helpful to us. Mr. La Rivière got us a room in a new hôtel run by a French couple. That, unfortunately, prevented us from meeting Joseph Kessel whom Henry de Montfreid had set up in a rival hôtel run by Greeks. The fierceness and joviality of this Russian guy, who sang at the top of his lungs and, after finishing his drink, smashed his glass against the walls and windows, made us want to know him.

Thanks to friends of my mother-in-law who let me shop at very reasonable prices, I was able to fill my steamer trunks with beautiful outfits from Philippe and Gaston, famous couturiers and furriers in the 1930s. My wardrobe would garner many compliments. As expected, the "King of Kings'" coronation lasted for days and attracted various celebrities and wealthy tourists in addition to the official representatives from all over the world, with whom we participated in the festivities.

Such was the case of Lady Ravensdale, the daughter of an Indian Viceroy, who came with her lover and an old American millionairess they met on the boat. They were staying at our hôtel and much preferred the comfort of our Citroën automobile to the dirty, expensive local taxis, to attend the numerous official ceremonies.

We also met a gentleman from the Basque region, Mr. Garicoix, and his wife, who were hired by the "Negus", the Emperor, to create and run two French high schools. They immediately adopted us with warm affection.

As conscientious in their work as Pierre, loyal and devoted, they were treasured friends. Jeanette Garicoix, fond of gossip, never let slip by a chance to bring us up to date on the latest. That, in fact, is how we learned we were envied because the French mission had leaked the financial arrangements of Pierre's contract. He took it very seriously whereas I made fun of it to the point that I wrote "Gossip under Addis Ababa's tin roofs" though thereafter

I never had the courage to reread it.

From the first weeks there, we were both struck by the contrasts in this society. Coexistence of the medieval and modern, privilege and abject poverty, beggars and lepers, and criminals begging in the streets with rocks balanced on their heads.

Our daily life was also full of contrasts, simplicity during the day with women in linen jumpers or dresses and men in khaki or white cotton outfits and, in the evening, very sophisticated low cut gowns for the ladies and suits or uniforms with full regalia for the men.

Diplomatic courtesy also had its contrasts with its sly and intense intrigues, whether by the "ras" against the Emperor or among the tribal chiefs themselves, not to mention the veiled maneuvering of the Europeans to limit any one country over another from gaining influence with the Negus.

This was especially true of the Italians who were overly solicitous and with whom we had less than cordial relations. We knew their motives. They foresaw the conquest of Ethiopia which occurred in 1935. For example, there was an Italian company that had won a contract to build a radio transmitter station by lowballing the bid; they then attempted to recoup the real costs by overrunning their monthly budget. Pierre stood up for the Emperor despite the Italians' every effort to curry favor with him and even to convince me of their good faith. Their obsequiousness made me laugh.

On the other hand, with Hitler not yet in power, we had no problem with the Germans. And it was with the British mission that we had the best rapport. Even so, Sir Baston's intervention to convince the Negus to have Pierre lead the Ethiopian project to define the country's borders was not to Pierre's liking. Sir Baston so desired a competent engineer to collaborate with the English contingent! He even tried to convince Pierre by introducing him to the pleasures of lion hunting. But my husband was able to avoid the assignment. So Sir Baston got a German engineer to take his place; he was unfortunately shot and killed by an arrow fired by an Issa warrior seeking a wife, needing for that purpose a seventh dried penis to add to his necklace ...

During the period of 1930 - 1933, only the Americans had no agenda and the laid back attitude of their representatives was testament to that. For example, one of them photographed the interior of a "toucoule", a traditional round hut made of branches, in which he had taken up residence and sent it to his superiors, writing that his stipend didn't allow for more decent lodgings. Another, in the middle of a reception for the French Minister, gave a demonstration of his gymnastic skills, attired in his dinner jacket. During a semi-official party where everyone was dancing to the music of an excellent jazz orchestra, a third American made his entrance on a racehorse that was to defend its title the following day.

The French mission didn't escape gossip with the exception of the Minister and his wife who, approaching retirement, wanted nothing more than to win at bridge and save some of their stipend.

This parsimony struck Maréchal Franchet d'Esperey, France's representative to the "King of King's" coronation, who retaliated with military harshness. He didn't hesitate to serve the Minister's bubbly to the native servants and professional dancers while serving a fine champagne to his official guests in the decorated tent in the mission's park.

As in Madagascar, Pierre and I quickly looked into a more welcoming and picturesque milieu. We became friends with white Russians whom the Emperor had welcomed following the revolution. The welcome was tied to the fact that, prior to 1917, the ras sent their sons to military school in Russia, the ras and

Russians both being primarily Orthodox Christians.

Our friends made us see that after two years of patience, the Emperor stopped supporting them so benevolently and employed them at reduced salaries. This was perfectly in keeping with the image of Haile Selassie – the Nagadi of his kingdom – as the most merchant of merchants!

Named Tafari, he was the son of Makonnen, a great warrior and cousin of Emperor Menelik II. He was designated crown prince and regent in 1917 by Menelik's daughter, Empress Zaoditou. King in 1928, he was crowned Emperor under the name Haile Selassie in 1930. The direct heir to the throne was Lidj Yassou, a Muslim and ally of the Turks; he was removed by the clergy and ras in 1916. They crowned his aunt Empress Zaoditou and supported Ras Tafari while his rival, the direct descendant of Menelik, lived in an isolated chateau. Surrounded by pretty young women and abusing alcohol, the latter had an easy, if degrading, existence and enjoyed relatively humane treatment.

Haile Selassie attained membership for his country in the League of Nations, hoping to protect it from a new attack by Italy. He abolished slavery in 1924, at least in theory. Wanting to demonstrate his desire to civilize Ethiopia, he sought out European and American advisors and arranged their arrival prior to the coronation. He used their presence to burnish his image in the eyes of his official guests.

Haile Selassie wanted to modernize his country, a difficult task for this man who ran up against the will of those who had paved his way to the throne. The clergy and ras, conservative and uncultured, refused change. Not powerful enough to enforce his own will, since certain of the ras such as Hailou had fortunes bigger than his own, the Negus had to constantly maneuver.

When the Italians invaded in 1935 with their modern tanks and planes, Badoglio quickly crushed the Ethiopians who were courageous but ill equipped. Haile Selassie fled to England while Hailou flirted with the enemy.

Some years later, the English occupied enough of the country that the Italians fled and Haile Selassie, who had been in Khartoum since 1941, regained his throne and held it until the 1974 revolution which had been preceded by numerous troubles.

Running up constantly against the ras' and lesser chieftains' greed and ignorance, always demanding bribes from the foreign companies which sought to exploit the mineral riches and would leave the country gutted, Haile Selassie never achieved his goal of bringing prosperity to his people.

As soon as we arrived in the country, Pierre met the Minister of Public Works, a ras, a noble gentleman, intelligent and likeable but unschooled. Luckily he was assisted by Ethiopian students from the Catholic mission schools, white Russian engineers and Germans who had been bankrupted in WWI. Pierre quickly established himself, as much by his charisma as his training. Thanks to the linguistically gifted white Russians, my husband was kept up to date on all the intrigues. Thus he was able to alert the French Minister of Italian encroachments at the Ethiopian border. Meanwhile, the French commandant and military attaché, who was funded to get news from the natives, preferred to pocket the money and play bridge.

Pierre was equally surprised by the rustic nature of his first project, enlarging the orthodox cathedral for the coronation festivities. This was accomplished using an enormous scaffold covered in Indian canvas dyed yellow. The beams consisted of long logs roughly stripped of their branches, simply attached by large nails. This primitive scaffold dressed in its fabric tent, gold in the ambient light, accentuated the clergy's sumptuous costumes and the gold embroidered capes of the other dignitaries. Despite their suits and uniforms with all their medals, the Europeans made a paltry impression. Only the women, thanks to the haute French couture, worn not only by the French ladies but all the European women, redeemed the decorum of the Western world.

After the festivities, Pierre continued to run up against an underfunded budget and the whims of the Emperor who could not reconcile his yearnings for magnificence with his finances. As was the custom, each Emperor had to build seven churches during his reign and Haile Selassie decided that his would be on the model of our gothic cathedrals even though the construction of roads essential to the economy should have taken precedence. Pierre managed to convince him to at least develop low cost trails usable eight months of the year.

The coronation festivities having had us in pleasant overdrive, I suddenly became exhausted and out of breath in the 8200 foot altitude. Nausea clearly alerted me to another pregnancy and many health nuisances unsettled my daily life. The Italian doctor quite rightly ordered me to the hospital as I neared my delivery date. This was not the natural childbirth I had experienced with Annette. The surgeon had to intervene. Florence joined our family to Annette's great joy; she had awaited her sister impatiently. Eight months later, one evening, feeling fatigued, I confided to Pierre my worries about the future and the care of my children. He gently chided me but awoke the next morning to find me unconscious at his side in the bed. I had a terrible case of malaria and my heart, hampered by the altitude, was failing. Pierre was very attentive, leaving his office every two hours to come to my bedside to give me my medicines. Oddly, when I was eighteen and in perfect health, Lucien Capet, the celebrated violinist and brother-in-law of my aunt Riquette, had predicted what would befall me in Ethiopia. His prediction was precise: "A crisis, potentially fatal if your will is not strong, will happen when you are about thirty, following the birth of your second child, far away, overseas, and after months of rest." I was twenty-seven and a half. Since arriving in Addis Ababa I had to rest all day to be in good form for the obligatory evenings of official receptions. The prediction came back to me. A fatalist, I accepted what seemed to me to be inevitable, all the while searching among our acquaintances for who would be a good spouse for Pierre and mother for our children. I was saved at death's door, without a doubt, by my husband's will and my doctor's knowhow. Our life went back to normal.

As the city was quite sprawling, Annette had to go to school on horseback, accompanied by a boy or young servant. One day she came home breathless, telling me a policeman had taken the boy and the horse on the pretext that he had seen them galloping which, according to my daughter, was false. She had barely finished telling me when a police officer arrived, demanding 18 thalers to get back the boy and the horse. Knowing from our Greek and white Russian friends the methods of the poorly paid police to get bribes for this or that, I refused to pay and lodged a complaint. Annette had to testify and immediately recognized the guilty officer when presented with a lineup of seven. Because of Pierre's distinguished position, the officer got three months in prison.

In turn, I suffered my own humiliation in the street, something that would have been unimaginable in Madagascar in 1930. I was on foot not far from the house, going to place an order at the market. I was walking on a narrow curb at the side of a wide road, little more than a gulley studded with pointed rocks. A very elegant native man mounted the curb headed in the opposite direction. I didn't pay it any notice at first, certain he would step down to let me pass, but he wasn't having any of it. So there we were, face to face, amid a hostile crowd that was watching with undisguised pleasure. It was I who, mortified, finally let him pass.

Pierre found himself in a similar situation. When they saw him alone at the wheel of his car, several Ethiopians spat on his path. The old-timers of the French mission explained this behavior: by going out without our servants we had not upheld our social station. It was a valuable lesson and, from then on, even if we only wanted to venture out for a short walk with Annette in the evening, we walked surrounded by a servant holding a lantern, another with a gun, one to hold our jackets, and Annette's nanny.

In town, the chiefs, accompanied by three or four family members and fifty-odd soldiers or servants added to the traffic jams. The richest of them, ras Hailou, went so far as to surround himself with three thousand warriors. When two ras or even two chieftains encountered each other, they would hail each other many times from their mounts, then dismount and continue their elaborate salutations. Dressed in white tunics covered by black cloaks, they all carried a concealed pistol that never left their person. For major ceremonies, their gold embroidered capes gave off a fiery sparkle while their mules competed with the glamour of their medieval-style harnesses. Although outlawed by the Emperor, Talion Law (an eye for an eye retribution), persisted in its ravages. One night we dined at the home of a doctor to whom was brought a man who had suffered about forty stab wounds. After having been saved with great difficulty, he had no sooner left than he attacked his assailant, wounding him twice as many times. The same held for traffic accidents but, in their case, the retribution was more likely to take the form of staggering sums of money: a native seeking to exorcise his inner demons would throw himself under a car, preferably owned by a European, to get money for the injuries he sustained, a practice we found throughout Eastern countries.

The Ethiopians considered themselves a conquering people who did not bow to menial tasks. During the first five months of our stay, we sublet a large villa with a dozen servants and horses from an Englishman who was away on leave. Despite the number of servants, I learned I had to reimburse the cook's delivery charges. To justify this expense, the cook explained that, having been born on the plateau, as was the rest of the staff, he had to engage the services of a "Gourague", a seasonal worker from the country, to carry the bags from the market. So when we finally took possession of the house we had restored and which I, once more, decorated according to my designs, I decided to reduce the number of servants to seven, making sure to include a Gourague for the menial tasks. At the end of a year, I once again noticed delivery charges for the cook. To my great surprise I learned that after a year's service in my house, the Gourague's status had become elevated and we needed someone to do his work! A very pretty young mulatto woman in our crowd, whose father was white Russian and mother a noble Ethiopian, one day told me how she had become a slave to the slaves. She married a wealthy ras and had a huge household of 500 servants. Custom required that she take responsibility for their and their children's food and health, and provide each two shirts per year. It is not so in the countryside, where the ras heavily taxed their people. They also failed to send their annual tithe to the Emperor. The Negus, however, an adept monarch, waited for the propitious moment to invite the ras to the capital where they paid their dues and a heavy fine for the oversight.

Protected by a succession of circular walls, the "Guebi" or imperial palace, was constructed merely of rudimentary shanties with the exception of the huge dining hall and the throne room whose walls were alternately decorated with Sèvres porcelain vases and non-functioning loudspeakers. Upon arriving, we would line up to greet their majesties, the Emperor, the Empress, and their youngest son, all three solemnly seated on an elevated crimson throne. Ladies curtseyed while men bowed respectfully. Even if it was good form to be somewhat blasé coming to these receptions or those of an important ras, there was no question that one had to attend. We knew any absence would be remarked and speculated about ad infinitum. The Emperor himself noticed the no-shows to these formal and boring parties and he looked upon them harshly. Besides the Emperor's excellent cuisine accompanied by his private label Mumm champagne, one of the entertaining pastimes was to observe the faux pas of certain greetings. One hilarious instance was the attendance by a Swedish colleague of Pierre, very fat, who bowed three times to their highnesses, completely unaware of his open trouser fly right under the Empress's nose! The latter, a very heavy woman, older than the Emperor and selected because she was a widow whose fertility was proven, remained inscrutable in the face of this most indecorous greeting.

The announcement of the screening of a film at one of these events was cause for rejoicing for those of us who were missing the theater and cinema. Unfortunately, the film was inevitably propaganda for Haile Selassie.

One day we attended the wedding of the crown prince. In love with a young woman his own age whom he knew from school, he had to submit to the will of the government and marry a woman he didn't love. Not familiar with European ways, his father-in-law offered salted Arabic coffee to his guests whose comical grimaces gave away their surprise.

Corpulence is a sign of wealth and nobility for Ethiopian women. The wife of the Minister of Public Works, a woman with regular features, was no exception to this rule. A shrewd mistress of her household, she herself offered us the first taste of a very spicy goulash rolled in a buckwheat crepe. The goal was to encourage the guests to drink with gusto the beer that was being served for the occasion to liven things up.

It was considered poor taste to discuss important matters – European or local – at this type of get-together. Besides, world events were pretty worrisome with the rise of Nazism and Mussolini's ambitions directed specifically at Ethiopia; a fluctuating French franc was eroding France's prestige, amplified by the stability of the pound sterling and a French government represented by the evil Laval who supported Mussolini.

Apparently imperturbable, the Negus, a horse-racing enthusiast, spent many Sundays at the track where, naturally, all international society was expected to be in attendance. It was a chance for the ladies to wear their new couture items that had arrived from France. It was also a venue that allowed the Europeans and Ethiopians to mingle.

Having finally moved into our new home, we organized a housewarming party with costumes required. A committee was set up to tally votes for the prettiest, funniest and most original costumes. I bought whimsical items from an elegant Russian boutique to serve as prizes for the eventual winners – wallets, necklaces and lighters. With great secrecy we decided with some friends to form a group dressing as characters from stories by Perrault (the original author of many of Grimm's fairy tales). Annette made a charming Little Red Riding Hood, while Pierre was a superb Bluebeard with seven miniature wives and an Ethiopian scimitar hanging at his side. The son of the French Minister, short in stature, made a perfect Puss 'n Boots. As for me, I was the Magic Donkey thanks to a Belgian friend, an import/export agent, who gave me a grey leather hide. He tailored it in such a way that it made a cape attached to a donkey's head, allowing a fairy-like, diaphanous golden tulle to peek through. The dress had a fiery red corsage sewn by Madame Konovaloff, a very dear Russian friend.

Our guests also showed their competitive skills. The Italians were irresistible poets and musicians. One, a kind of futuristic artist, was a Picasso-like sculpture with a tilting breast and an exclamation point between his legs. A Russian advertised the event wearing a sandwich board decorated with spiritual sketches depicting our guests as animals. Added to all this were more traditional costumes, authentic all the same.

The Belgian Minister, an important and distinguished man, having refused to come in costume, was selected as head of the voting committee. I had great difficulty declining the prize for the most beautiful costume, which would have been ridiculous for the organizer of the party. They finally wound up electing a ravishing French woman in authentic Indian dress who was close behind me in votes.

I also have a fond memory of another very different party at the home of friends, at which Henry de Montfreid was present. At the time, he was the touted novelist of the day, possessing the talent to unmask the secrets and savagery of the banks of the Red Sea ... The ironic and spiritual theories of this arms and drug dealer amused us. The cynicism that propelled him to add a moral at the end of each chapter – for the sole purpose of pleasing his admirers – astonished us.

The vicissitudes of his existence were bizarre. The English and French both put a price on his head during WWI for having supplied arms to Germany. More recently, a man he wanted done away with set off with him on his boat from Obock, but was nowhere to be found upon the boat's arrival in Djibouti. Before fleeing to avoid prison yet again, he stayed on board because the port was guarded, the police observing him from the docks. On watch from his dhow, he spotted the governor of Djibouti and his wife both watching the action. He gleefully told us how, at age fifty-five and knowing his arrest was imminent, he had removed his pants and mooned the governor.

His hearing, held in Montpelier, resulted in a release order. He was acquitted because friends had destroyed compromising papers that had been on the boat. When his lawyer cabled him the good news and spared him as well from eight days in a "corcoro" prison with 115 degree Fahrenheit temperatures, he refused to pay for the telegram! As the bread and electricity supplier for the region of Harrar and the town of Diredawa, he was very rich, but his greed had no equal except his sense of adventure.

This fellow was finally exiled by the Negus for selling arms simultaneously to the French Somalis and their rival Ethiopian Somali tribe, thus setting off a horrific conflict. But things didn't stop there. The French sent a warship and some planes to protect its enclave around Djibouti, which angered the Emperor, who considered the action a challenge. The Negus blamed de Montfreid who, furious, published a series of successful articles. He lost his right of residence in Ethiopia.

We met him again many years later in Montmartre, as ever, between adventures. This time he confided his intention to offer his services to Mussolini to recoup his wealth. We were shocked. And the way he treated his wife, a German we had never met, was mind-boggling: he made her travel third class with the crush of bushmen whose practice was to smear their hair with rancid butter, giving off an unbearable odor.

A French doctor friend of his, who treated the Montfreid family at no cost, received in exchange watercolors painted by Henry whose modest talent was in sharp contrast to his strong personality. When the doctor died suddenly, leaving his wife and children in need, the French Consul tried to help them by selling anything of worth at the highest possible price to the French colony. He received a letter from Montfreid who dared, to everyone's surprise, to demand back his paintings which had risen in value as a result of his fame as a writer. The pettiness of this charming and talented man would remain an eternal mystery to me.

Wanting at all costs to experience the wild bushland, I accompanied my husband on a work excursion. Following a preliminary report by two German engineers, he had to choose the exact route of a road and bridge. The departure was by truck along the section of the road that already existed. We then went on by mule, but several had died, decimated by bites from tsetse flies which we would encounter again in the Omo valley. Thus the caravan made its way with the mules and luggage at the lead. We followed with the ascaris, or guards, and some servants. While fording a stream, our sleeping cots fell into the water, so we spent the first night on our straw mattresses, attacked by bed bugs. The caravan got under way again the next morning. Designated servants went ahead to put up the tents and buy food from the villagers. On this dry and barren soil we observed beautiful gazelles framed by the sky or leisurely romping.

I particularly enjoyed dawn when one awoke to fragrant nature with the antelopes like shadow puppets. Occasionally during the trip a huge tree rising in the grassland would offer a refreshing rest stop in the shade.

Little by little, we approached the Omo valley, reputed to be dangerous not only because of the tsetse fly but also because of the number of robbers based there to attack caravans. We decided to leave the tents and the animals on the plateau and descend the 2000 feet to the river below, obscured by plants that were taller than we were. We discovered, in a wood thick with brush, a number of wild animals. Some black and white monkeys cavorted in the trees above large water buffalo with huge horns. Alas, an engineer fired his pistol by accident and sent fleeing the hundred or so beasts we had been admiring with marvel.

Fatigued from the heat and beckoned by the coolness of the river, I decided to take a swim. Not having brought a bathing suit, I put on a pair of Pierre's pajamas in which I literally floated. Two servants immediately took charge of me, supporting me at the elbows. Out of respect, they wore black jackets, totally out of place in this savage environment – all the more so since they weren't long enough to cover their private parts which floated under my nose as I tried to swim! On the shore, Pierre delighted at my predicament.

Later in the afternoon, we headed back. Our guides were unsure of the way. Weariness began to slow our steps and we decided to kill a water buffalo as we had no more food. Pierre finally hit an antelope, his shot striking the animal in the anus; one of the boys finished it off with a knife. Our men immediately tasted our prey, taking the warm meat in their bare hands. We did the same to regain our strength. This meat without salt was sickening.

The trip resumed. The night allowed us to make out shining eyes all around. It was impossible to know what animals they belonged to. Some of the men shivered with fear, worrying about sorcerers, spirits, thieves or wild animals. Our white companions dreaded the leopard, a ferocious beast that attacks when injured. But I, completely enthralled by the disquieting mystery, was not afraid, earning me the title Gobese woman, which signifies courage and strength.

Here and there, the lights flickered, encircling us. It was impossible to know what creatures were doing this. Around midnight we finally arrived at camp, exhausted. During the night, gunshots caused us to rush from the tents. Our guards had shot at audacious hyenas which, despite the protective fires we had lit, were attacking the mules.

The following day, near the village, on our return path, our interpreters were buying chickens from some women gathered at the base of two huge trees. I was admiring their silver arm and ankle ornaments. Suddenly, they squealed when they noticed my blond hair beneath my hat, my engagement ring and a small brooch fastening the collar of my blouse. My riding breeches and sweater had disguised my femininity rather well. They inspected every aspect of me because it was the first time they had seen a white woman and they laughed out loud over every little thing such as my watch. It was too brief an encounter!

Not wanting to take advantage of my sex, I rode the mules only when spent, as I usually was at the end of a day's march. Approaching our resting place, I heard shouts and saw a local armed with a knife ready to skewer our cook. My scream stopped him. Thanks to my husband's intervention, the hostile crowd finally agreed to sell us some food. We later understood the reason for their behavior: they feared the future road going through their lands. French peasants would have reacted the same way.

As a precaution, we decided to keep the village chief at the camp in one of the tents. We went to bed well fed and satisfied. At dawn, loud cries roused us from bed. The chief had escaped and our men were running to look for him. As I followed them toward the village, the locals started pelting us with stones. The women were screaming their heads off: "Gouragues, Gouragues"! While recapturing the chief we noticed a long column of men, guns in hand, ammunition across their chests, visible despite their black capes with pointed hoods. It was nerve-racking.

The Germans, used to the bush, reassured us by explaining that the ammunition rarely matched the caliber of the gun. The Gouragues approached and saw their chief in the firm custody of our ascaris. The time to talk had come. Pierre explained that he was Emperor Haile Selassie's representative. One of the engineers translated "In opposing our presence, you are attacking the

Emperor. We will do anything it takes to respect your lands. We will take your chief to Addis Ababa to be judged".

Pierre's brief remarks had an immediate effect on the villagers' attitude which went from hostile to submissive. All the able-bodied men assisted in taking down the tents and were zealous enough to help me mount my mule, putting their hands on my buttocks. Looking as if I might protest, a man in the know advised that I not refuse this sign of respect.

And so our caravan departed, noticeably longer than before as the whole village, including women and children, had fallen into step with us. This did not fail to cause serious problems even as early as the first rest stop, having to keep everyone fed. At the end of the day, a delegation of village women came to me, genuflecting and kissing my feet, begging for mercy for their chief. We were only too happy to grant it, since it would greatly lighten our load.

A new surprise awaited me at the next village where a great Muslim chief offered us the hospitality of his beautiful hut. In accordance with the custom of his household, he tasted everything first to prove he wasn't trying to poison us, then gave me a glass of the juice of a sugar cane he had peeled with his teeth. I passed it to Pierre and he gave it to the engineers. The chief then asked our interpreters a question. They laughed and looked embarrassed but didn't translate. I insisted so they said "Okay, he says he is very rich, that he owns the whole village and the fields, and he offers a hut to each of his wives". "Is that what made you laugh?" I asked. "He also wants to know how much you cost".

I flinched, disgusted at the idea of this old coots' desire and made everyone leave immediately despite how tired the men were. Later on, I regretted my stubborn insistence, fired by my vivid imagination.

In the same spirit and during the same trip, I remember with some shame wanting, for a brief moment, to buy a young girl, for artistic purposes only, her beauty giving the impression of pure perfection. I regretted it as one regrets missing out on a piece of art. I had not taken up my brushes in a long time.

The end of our expedition was drawing near and I was anxious to rejoin my children whom we had left with our friends, the Garicoix. Knowing Annette's stubborn nature, I anticipated some comments. True to form, she had shown her personality, strong and determined, not afraid to stand up to adults. By contrast, Florence, sweet and easy, really liked our friend who was also her godfather...

During our three year stay in Addis Ababa, my health was not up to par. More comfortable at 6000 feet or lower altitude, as the Omo expedition had shown, after Florence's birth I spent a month in Diredawa at 5000 feet. It was a great stay for my daughters, punctuated by weekend visits from Pierre. To make the return easier, we also took repeated trips to the home of a German farmer at 6000 feet. This man was the first to make us realize the Nazi danger in 1932, a year before Hitler's election: "If the Fuhrer calls us to wage war, I'll be the first to go" he said.

When the Emperor asked if Pierre would like to come back following a respite in France, the answer was negative. The altitude didn't agree with me and my husband realized he was overqualified for his role there. Despite the French Minister's assertion that he should expect a delay of six months to receive his pay, Pierre had no problem getting it two months prior to the end of his contract. We left a small bonus for our household staff based on a thaler for each month they had been with us. Our boy wanted to accompany us as far as Djibouti which really touched us. The Minister of Public Works hurried, late as usual, running the length of the train which was slowly pulling out, to have Pierre sign some official papers. As was the custom at Antananarivo, our friends and acquaintances all turned out to see us off.

We stayed for three days in Djibouti waiting for the ship to Marseille. My mother and Clotilde were waiting for us at the port and we learned my mother-in-law had had a stroke. She rallied a bit with our surprise visit to Cier where she was staying but several other strokes followed, progressively diminishing her faculties during six long years. After reuniting with family, Pierre went to Paris to make his report and submit his bids for a new posting.

I keep a wonderful memory of the beautiful legend of the imperial dynasty formed by the marriage of King Solomon and the Queen of Sheba. The dynastic line was broken when Haile Selassie was imprisoned by rebels in 1974 and eventually died.

The legend tells the story of the Queen's journey in Judea, sumptuously awaited by King Solomon. Alarmed by her host's heavy drinking, she sends a servant in her place to him during the night, then changes her mind when the servant returns, captivated. The myth explains the double line of descent to which is credited this enduring dynasty.

Ethiopian painters repeat the theme over and over on the cotton canvases, the "aboudjedid".

These works also depicted major battles, notably the first at Adoua in 1896 which concluded in Menelik's victory over General Baratieri, illustrating the victors cutting the penises of the vanquished. Mussolini took revenge for a short period in 1935; the May 1941 English victory restored Haile Selassie to the throne.

From 1974 until the collapse of communism in Europe, a succession of revolutionaries, trained and equipped by the USSR, killed each other and massacred students. Long independent, Ethiopia, in majority Orthodox Christian, enjoyed a certain leadership among the members of the Organization for African Unity, which endured until the fall of the Negus. It has never regained its prominent place.

FOUR

THE PHONY WAR
OF 1939-1940

Convinced since our return from Ethiopia that war was inevitable, we decided to take advantage of the peaceful time that remained. We wouldn't regret it as we had underestimated what was to come: lightning fast defeat, humiliating Nazi occupation, torture, raging racism and the death of our fellow Resistance fighters.

Pierre accepted a two year assignment as Secretary General of Roads and Bridges, poorly paid but not too demanding, which allowed him to reclaim his place in the ordered old school of strict practices, a contrast to the whims of the Negus, authoritarian, lucid and capricious.

For the third time in our marriage, I set out in search of a home, funded by the proceeds from the sale of our furniture and automobile in Ethiopia, about 55,000 francs.

Faithful to the principles of my dear professor of design, Dr. Burkalter, who liked to say "No faux antiques, no lazy way out", I looked for unique furnishings created by artisans who had the courage to create, not imitate. The charm of contemporary

furniture having been lost in mass production, I instead opted for
prototype pieces from traveling exhibitions. I kept them for a long
time and some pieces still grace my apartment in Monaco.

Following my doctor's advice, we decided to wait a year before
having a third child. Our wish was granted and Didier, our first
son, was born in a maternity clinic in the XIVth arrondissement of
Paris. The baby joyously sucked on the cork of the champagne
tasted in his honor and quickly became known as "Rizou" because
he laughed constantly. He was easy and lovable and made a great
trio with his older sisters Annette and Florence. This did not
prevent the latter from unconscious jealousy and a sad face. One
day at nap time, I pulled her to me and kissed her. She said "Kiss
Rizou, too!". "No, it's you I am kissing; he's happy, you see, he's
smiling" I replied. "One can be smiling and still suffer when one's
mother kisses another child" she retorted. Flo's observation, at
four years old, will be forever etched in my memory. She would
choose to pursue psychology at the age of seventeen.

Our savings from Ethiopia allowed us to live above the means
of Pierre's salary and we did not hesitate to enjoy the pleasures of
Paris. Our favorite entertainment was attending dances where we
found people different from our usual crowd. There were
professional dancers, rich old ladies or younger kept women who
enjoyed dancing with men their own age, and people from the
provinces looking for excitement. Watching them on the dance
floor, we amused ourselves by trying to imagine their lives and
inventing encounters stemming from little nothings. As for us, we
let ourselves go with the current dances and the rhythm of the
orchestra. The live music allowed the musicians to prolong a
selection as they wished, in response to the grace and intimacy of
one or several couples. They often did it for us because we took
lessons to learn the new dances each time we returned from the
tropics. Even for the most trivial things, Pierre was a perfectionist.

We were eclectic in our selection of dancing venues, frequenting the most exclusive as well as the most working class spots such as the one in rue Rochechouart which featured two excellent orchestras. Perfect partners, we always went dancing by ourselves, preferring to see family and friends at artists' private parties, evenings of theater, or good restaurants.

Despite our joyful life in Paris, it was time for my husband to seek a more challenging assignment so as to move up to the level of chief engineer and earn a higher salary; the nest egg we had built up in the tropics was starting to seriously erode. I was thirty-two and considered myself old, and Pierre was thirty-nine. We left for Soissons with our two daughters, Annette and Florence, who were ten and five, respectively, and baby Didier, nine months old.

Before our arrival, an engineer picked out a villa to rent on a large boulevard. It was neither ugly nor beautiful, but comfortable and surrounded by gardens. We moved in right away, changing only the wallpaper.

Here as with every other place destiny would take us, we were accepted very quickly, thanks to Pierre's wit, our friendliness and also our love of dancing which was very common for women but less so among men.

We had barely arrived when we were invited to an official presentation, rather stuffy, in honor of the departing "sous-préfet", the county governor. Happily, Dr. Roy, the head of the hospital, an excellent surgeon and a bon vivant, made quick work of it. Realizing he had attended classes with Pierre at Fontainebleau in 1917, he called out to him familiarly, "Do you remember the nights we slept together and had to go out the window to take a piss?".

Our friendship lasted many long years during which I always appreciated the surgeon's humor and the intelligence of his wife, Jeanne.

The Deshayes, another couple, with boys the same age as Annette and Florence, were also longtime friends. He was a landscape architect specializing in gardens, a tall, calm, good looking man and his wife was petite, lively and smart. This friendship, like that with Dr. Roy, would extend through our children and grandchildren.

Quickly settling into the rhythm of the small town of Soissons, we always loved to go dancing and play tennis. In summer, we went regularly to the outdoor pool near the river Aisne in a park-like area dedicated to all types of sports. Taking an interest in young swimmers and their progress, Pierre even became president of this small local club.

But the arrival of a new "sous-préfet" and, especially, his spouse, would cast a shadow on our relationship. Small, cultured and finicky, he was constantly berated by his wife, statuesque and a bit heavy, with a fine wit but very bossy. She dominated us, pushed herself into our group and, needless to say, had us all marching to her orders.

Having instantly recognized her personality, I tried in vain to fend off this dominatrix. Pierre was carried away by the continuous advances from this beautiful, proud woman. And when, exasperated, I spoke to him about it, he replied that, as a civil servant, he was obliged to maintain excellent relations with the "sous-préfet" – and his wife. As is the case for many women confronted by this situation, I suffered greatly from this "friendship" which would cause me to lose forever the naive confidence and excessive admiration I had for Pierre. In hindsight, it made me find within myself a strength that would be invaluable. Without wanting to dwell on it, I can't gloss over this episode in our lives.

These few prewar years in Soissons were soon interrupted by the 1938 call to arms during which Pierre was commissioned commandant of an artillery battery at Troyes. When, after fifteen days he returned, I called this episode "la guerre de Troie n'aura pas lieu" ("Tiger at the Gates" by Giraudoux), recalling the play. Didier, three years old, called it "Papa's little war".

Dismayed by the Munich Agreement, we knew full well this backing down would serve Germany more than France.

In "Mein Kampf", Hitler had made his maneuvers and attacks on coveted countries clear but none of the heads of state involved had the courage to defend Czechoslovakia, to join together to prevent the destruction of Europe and the Soviet Union.

Thus war broke out on September 1, 1939. Jacques Deshayes and Pierre were the only ones mobilized among our middle class crowd in Soissons. I received a letter every day from my husband who was at the front at the Siegfried line.

After an unexpected trip to fulfill a secret mission in our area – during which he could not, despite my pleas, refrain from visiting the "sous-préfet"'s wife – Pierre disappeared again. He returned to the front where the main attack was imminent. Belgium had already been invaded and the German army was preparing to advance over open terrain to Holland.

Quickly France was in free fall. Panic was widespread and our troops were retreating, weighed down by their weapons, through town to escape toward the south. As much as I and Mesdames Deshayes and Roy wanted to stay and tend to the refugees from the department of Aisne sheltered at the train station, the male contingent, particularly Dr. Roy and Mr. Eugene Touzé, made us leave town.

First the children and the maid, Marie-Rose, were evacuated in the middle of the night en route to Cier-de-Rivière where my invalid mother-in-law had already arrived. I joined them a few days later. My adventure on the road in the south was like those of all the French – we were traumatized by the sudden defeat and didn't understand what was happening. General de Gaulle's June 18, 1940 appeal gave me great comfort.

For his part, Pierre was pulling back, step by step, with General Frère's army, from Holland to the Massif Central in south-central France. He had already received a medal for a dangerous mission in Normandy during which his friend, Jacques Deshayes, was taken prisoner.

Irritable and distressed, he joined us at Cier-de-Rivière. I welcomed him with a spouse's comforting love. Given the circumstances, I felt I was the stronger one and, while taking care of Pierre and the children, I was determined to help the Resistance as soon as I could find a contact. Without telling me, Pierre had the same idea. Being Jewish and not wanting to be a burden to my husband, I waited for him to let me in on his thoughts. But he quickly had to leave to take up a new assignment as Chief Engineer at Laon where he joined the Resistance. He sent us the "Ausweis" or travel documents so we could join him.

The return to Soissons was not very joyous. After a thorough cleaning of the villa, defiled to the point of nausea by the Germans who were still stationed on the ground floor, we reoccupied only the three rooms on the second floor. We didn't even have use of the kitchen.

At the urging of the "sous-préfet"'s wife, we accepted, along with the Roys whose house had also been partly occupied, her offer to share our meals at her house. Each of the women used her personal contacts to get food for all.

Living in Laon, Pierre returned to Soissons on weekends but soon had to flee to Paris, fearing he had been marked by the Gestapo. Thus began for us a series of difficult adventures in connection with the Resistance.

FIVE

THE EARLY YEARS OF THE RESISTANCE

One morning in October 1943, Pierre returned to our apartment at 60 rue de la Tourelle in Boulogne, a suburb of Paris. I sensed he had something to tell me but was holding back. He waited until the children were asleep before finally telling me:

"I had a meeting this afternoon with a comrade, an important Resistance leader, at the corner of boulevard Malesherbes and the rue d'Anjou. Three men in raincoats stopped me, calling me M. Taille and explaining that they had come in place of a certain M. Dufor. Right away I was worried and replied that I was not this gentleman and had a date with a woman who had obviously stood me up. My briefcase was full of compromising documents. I slowly walked away with measured steps so they would not sense my haste. I learned later in the afternoon that Dufor (Resistance alias of Roland Farjon) disappeared two days ago. He was arrested so the identity of these men leaves no doubt: they were Gestapo."

"Taille, your Resistance name, is known!", I replied.

A long conversation ensued. We tried to assess the danger

without exaggerating it. Spent with emotion but unburdened of his tale, Pierre finally went to sleep. During the many months to come, he would feel spied upon and suspect ambushes, yet he would never abandon his clandestine struggle against the enemy.

Each week I waited with growing impatience for the Saturday evenings when he would return to Boulogne, a suburb of Paris, to our small apartment. But I couldn't resist calling him every day at Laon where he carried out his duties as Chief Engineer of Roads and Bridges and as a Resistance fighter. The former was beneficial for the latter.

Work-related field trips allowed for observing the military throughout the region. Very few subordinates knew the real identity of their Chief Engineer, head of the Resistance for the departments of Aisne and Ardennes. They liked and respected their superior not knowing he was one of the members of the board of the "Organisation Civile et Militaire" (OCM), a Resistance movement that would become famous following the Liberation.

Pierre returned each week a little more tired and a little more worried. All phone calls were monitored. Arrests mounted up. The atmosphere was oppressive. Did these developments possibly stem from Dufor's arrest? The question was posed. Many documents must have been found at his house. Serious suspicion of betrayal also fell on his shoulders.

The Pas-de-Calais department had just had numerous victims. A huge cache of weapons had been discovered. In that area, the name Dufor was frequently mentioned. Had he talked? What torture had they subjected him to? He was said to be condemned to death but no one knew any details.

At the end of December, Pierre arrived home upset. A number of arrests had taken place in his region, notably among his crew. Many were able to evade the roundup but one, distraught at being taken, committed suicide that night. Bertin, my husband's friend, father of six, had had to flee and the Gestapo was already at his home. Should Pierre return to Laon or should he hide out with a false identity and abandon the official post so useful to his clandestine activities?

We quickly came to agreement. An escape seemed necessary but, to set it up, he asked for medical leave and went once more to his office. This return to Laon, quick as it was, was extremely dangerous. I endured four days of anguish.

This well organized ruse worked out well but it didn't go far enough. Pierre had to cut contact with me and change his identity. I removed all his medals and insignia – Legion d'Honneur, old and new "croix de guerre", from all his jackets. We carefully removed his monogram from his hat, underwear and wallet. Pierre became André Moreau.

A kind and courageous friend got him a cover job at his company and put him up for a while. But separation was hard and Pierre came sometimes like a thief in the night to see his family.

"You are the best Gestapo agent" he said one evening to little Olivier, born May 9, 1943. "You are going to get me captured".

Shared between my husband and four children, I used every trick to avoid being followed when I would go to bring him his messages that came via our maid, Jeannine, a veritable living post box.

Our meeting locations were quite varied until I found him a small workman's lodging in the rue Amelot. The concierge thought we were an unorthodox couple. It would serve us well. It explained perfectly why we were out of step with this blue collar area.

One day, a woman came to the house to interview me about the Red Cross which I found odd. I was suspicious of her. Four days later, two big fellows asked the concierge where we lived.

The switchboard operator for the building had just enough time to alert me before the men rang the doorbell. I even managed to hide some papers before opening the door. They said they were insurance agents and wanted to know if my husband was home...

Knowing the Gestapo checks usually came in threes, I expected another visit for which I did not have to wait long. The doorbell at 7:30 a few mornings later brought another "insurance agent".

I learned much later from the German military police that my husband had been sought since November by the Gestapo service at rue des Saussaies.

Despite all this, Pierre worked more and more for the Resistance because he had the time. He replaced the Chief of the FFI (Forces Françaises de l'Intérieur, the Resistance's unified military forces) for the Paris region when that man was slaughtered in the street by the Germans who had come to arrest him. The mounting malaise gave rise to suspicion of a highly placed traitor, perhaps even in London. The losses were too great. Four of the seven directors of the OCM were already in prison. Pierre decided to launch a counter-espionage effort in the heart of the groups. The traitor was among them.

Suddenly awakened by the doorbell around midnight, I welcomed my sister-in-law and a doctor friend. They told me that I and the children had to leave immediately. A fuller explanation revealed that a Gestapo agent had tried to get Pierre's new address from his replacement at Laon. He even made known his intent to arrest and kill him. If not, he would arrest another family member.

The speed of one and all allowed the office chauffeur to forewarn the Chief Engineer in Soissons who fled to his sister's place in Paris. The latter, taking advantage of her medical credentials and their travel privileges for driving at night, arrived at my sister-in-law's, whose address was known in Laon, and then to my place.

Decisions had to be made quickly. With Easter vacation approaching, I used the most haste to get my three eldest children quickly away. Friends helped hide them. That very evening, I brought Pierre up to date on this new development.

Despite the danger, we made a plan to meet again the next day so Pierre could introduce me to André, his liaison officer. The arrest of one of us could be imminent and this young man could alert the other.

Following this meeting with André, Pierre was a bit worried. He found the young man's attitude strange. He insisted on paying for dinner and did not drink or smoke – a little suspect.

Having decided to stay at the apartment with the baby, who would perhaps help me avoid prison if arrested, I did a general inspection of the apartment, destroying or safeguarding with friends what I couldn't keep. I also put some papers in a utility room for which the key was held by the concierge. Pierre and Clotilde were the only ones who did not disapprove of my decision to stay on.

Having another rendezvous with Pierre at 7:30 p.m. in a small, discreet restaurant, I waited in vain until 9 p.m. I met up with my sister-in-law in the metro, having urgently called her. We shared our anxiety. The curfew prevented me from making a quick visit to the apartment in the rue Amelot so I went home to an evening of nightmares, imagining the worst, waiting for morning so I could go early to the rue Amelot.

The anxiety and fatigue got the better of me. I woke up a little late and, after taking care of Olivier and leaving him with the concierge, I didn't get to the apartment until after 10 a.m..

As soon as I got to the building's entry, the concierge came out of her place, completely unnerved. "Madame Moreau, if you knew what happened! ... Gestapo men were here hardly a half hour ago.

They came with four trucks and packed all Mr. Moreau's things in them."

I was devastated and returned home. I knew I, too, would be visited by the Gestapo. Had I been earlier, I might have been taken as an accomplice. Luck had served me but only me.

The first thing to do was warn friends who could be endangered as a result of Pierre's arrest. Then go home. If I went into hiding it would be impossible to take steps to help my imprisoned husband. I waited for the visit from these men which would not be a long wait.

At 6 p.m. I was at the home of a friend in the Resistance. At 7 p.m. I was at my sister-in-law's, at 9 p.m. at the home of the person who would receive our mail. I finally got home at 10 p.m. with my baby in my arms. I learned from the concierge that the men had already been there asking for me.

Falling asleep quickly after this arduous day, I was abruptly awakened around midnight by the doorbell. Three men burst in and turned over everything in their path. "Your husband is a terrorist. He is head of the Paris region."

The interrogation began. I was on the defensive. They vehemently accused me of being in on everything and of being the blonde who went regularly every Wednesday and Friday to the rue Amelot. I played dumb and started talking about a Vichy propaganda pamphlet I had purposely left on the table.

The interrogation resumed:

"Where were you at 7 p.m.?"

"At my sister-in-law's."

"Where does she live?"

"22 rue le Marois."

How lucky I was. I learned later that, after having missed me at my apartment, they had gone to my sister-in-law's where they observed me leaving. That made me appear forthright and innocent. After some words amongst themselves they decided not to bring me in right away, not knowing what to do with my baby. I was ordered to go to bureau 533 at the rue des Saussaies at 11 a.m. the next day.

First, I took the precaution of sending my concierge to the rue Amelot with the goal, aided by an envelope with money, of convincing the concierge there not to recognize me in the event of a confrontation. I also went to my sister-in-law's to ask her to keep her nephew, and to bring her up to date on what I had already told the Gestapo.

As soon as I arrived at the squalid bureau 533, I was sick to see French people going there as friends of the Germans. The atmosphere was awful and charged.

After an hour's wait, they made me pass through a men's cell where four poor souls were being held – haggard, unshaven, not daring to speak – before putting me in a disgusting cell on the ground floor. Was I to see Pierre as I had been led to believe? I hoped to and not at the same time. The desire to see him was negated by my fear of his torment at seeing me in this cursed place or to find him disfigured by mistreatment.

The heavy sounds of billy clubs, interspersed with cries and groans, came from neighboring cells and heightened my anxiety.

Thus I spent the day along with two other women with whom I talked, not without a bit of mistrust. One, the wife of a man who had escaped the STO, compulsory work in Germany, was incarcerated at the Fresnes prison. She was at bureau 533 for interrogation. The other, about twenty years old, was an unfortunate young woman who slept with Germans to make her living. Her soldier boyfriend, accused of selling his gun, was considered a deserter and they wanted to make his girlfriend talk. She wasn't having any of it.

Very late in the afternoon, one of the three men who had come to my apartment in the middle of the night sent me home with orders to return the next day at 8 a.m. I would wait many more hours to finally be interrogated. The bulk of the questions were the same as the first night, but posed differently; they could have tripped me up or made me contradict myself. I knew my role by heart. Still, my judge persisted:

"Useless to deny it. Your husband told us you were aware of his activities."

The ploy was classic and I was not falling for it.

"If my husband said such a false thing he must not be himself. What have you done to him?"

"Not at all. Your husband was interrogated here in this same office, seated like you on this chair."

These words seemed so sincere that I was somewhat reassured. Only a few months later, I would learn that one of his accomplices had tortured Pierre horribly.

The interrogation continued and I sensed that he believed I was innocent.

"You may leave" he said, finally…

"May I know where my husband is and may I bring him a package?"

"That depends. Was he arrested at home or elsewhere?"

"I have no idea. I only learned of his arrest from you."

"He is at Fresnes prison and you may bring him a package of up to 10 lbs."

The final trap was avoided. He knew a woman went to rue Amelot after the arrest and he suspected me, rightly so, of being that woman and thus aware of what had happened prior to their visit to my apartment.

A bit puzzled at having extricated myself so well, I left relatively relieved to know where Pierre was incarcerated and determined to bring him, as quickly as possible, a package that would link him again to his family.

Making the first trip that very evening to Fresnes, with my sister-in-law, we met other families as anxious as we were. We learned what approaches to take and what disappointments to fear … and the first was not long in coming. Pierre Pène was not known at Fresnes. I had no better luck trying André Moreau.

The quest was slow and painful. Returning tirelessly to Fresnes as well as to any office which could possibly give me information, I threw myself into the mystery. Pierre remained untraceable.

Prepared to do anything to achieve my goal, I went one day to the avenue Henri-Martin, to the home of a M. Palmieri, a former caretaker of brothels in Pas-de-Calais, whom I was told had an in with the Gestapo. Put in touch by a mutual acquaintance, I was immediately ushered in. After allowing me to speak he said, "You want to know where your husband is and to help him, But do you know why he is accused?"

"Not at all. But after what the Gestapo led me to believe, I have every reason to be worried."

"In that case, everything depends on his attitude and yours. I have the power to get him released from prison and placed in another Resistance group…"

"I don't understand" I said naively.

"It depends on his giving us the names of his comrades".

The proposition knocked the wind out of me and I bolted to my feet to leave immediately. Visibly moved to pity by my reaction, Palmieri allowed me to leave without further comment. He must have taken me for a fool.

A few days after the Liberation, by chance I heard talk of this cursed address, a hotbed of torture and death, where two Corsicans, of which one was Palmieri, worked in reality for the Germans. In the basement of this luxurious building, a room was littered with bloodstains and bullets.

The effort to find Pierre continued ... This time, I asked the Secretary General of the Ministry of Public Works to officially get involved in the search but to no avail. In fact, perhaps they did nothing?

After six weeks of waiting, I decided to make contact with the liaison officer, André, to whom Pierre had introduced me prior to his arrest. Clever tactics allowed me to meet with him. Another of Pierre's comrades, Dr. Mairesse, a.k.a. Hache, a father of three, disappeared about the same day. We would learn much later that the poor soul, with little air and no water, suffocated to death on a train that left Compiègne for Germany July 2, 1944; nine hundred other deportees succumbed to the same fate on that train.

Conscientiously, Clotilde and I sought out anyone who might help us, any new direction to take. Imperceptibly and inexplicably, our anxiety subsided a bit and, one Sunday, the doorbell rang.

Out of breath, Clotilde's concierge brought an envelope that had been delivered by two Germans. A response was required by 7 p.m. at the hôtel Edouard VII. It was a handwritten note from Pierre!

"I am in good health but very worried about my family. Give the bearer of this message the following items ... Be brave, I think of you a lot and love you."

What emotion! The packages so often prepared and dismantled for the last six weeks would finally be put to use. The best of everything we had was carefully wrapped in a fabric parcel. The children gave their chocolate rations, carefully saved for their father since his arrest. We also included photos of all of us, taken for this purpose and dated, to show that I was not in prison. The future was not clear but the present was beautiful.

The delivery of the package gave us no further information than the message. In front of the hotel where we waited, a man got out of a car to collect the package without saying a word…

It would be many more days of waiting before hearing from Pierre's lips the story told below and again over a dinner:

"I had a meeting at 10 a.m. with one of my Resistance comrades, Jacques, at the Sèvres-Babylone metro station. From there, we went quickly to the library in the rue d'Assas to check my false identity papers. In my briefcase, I was carrying three hundred thousand new francs to be distributed to the different Resistance cells, as well as compromising papers to be delivered to my liaison officer, who did not know the whereabouts of my hideout. Entering the porte cochère, I caught the gaze of the concierge but didn't register her terrified expression. When we got to the second floor, we realized the library was closed so we had to go back down to get the key. Just then, Jacques said to me "Two strange guys came in after us". He had hardly finished the sentence when five men surged in front of us, pistols in hand. Handcuffed from behind and punched in the head, we were thrown in two separate cars and taken at top speed to bureau 533, rue des Saussaies. Of course, my briefcase and datebook were confiscated. The interrogation began, brutal, interrupted by blows and other physical violence. My paramount concern was, of course, not to talk, to gain time to let comrades, unaware of my arrest, go into hiding. The Germans' techniques were aimed at making us lose our will, humiliating us with barbarous force, destabilizing us psychologically. They alternated interrogation with torture, followed by long periods of waiting in a "Bereitschaftszimmer" or preparation room, for an hour or even an entire day, from which we could hear the sounds of other comrades being similarly tortured.

The bathtub torture was particularly hard to endure. Seated with my back against the tub, I was first sprayed with cold water. When I refused to answer anything, I was turned over and submerged, feet in the air. I lost my breath, was suffocating, and furiously thinking what I could say that would not give up my comrades. Immersed for dozens of seconds, I began to lose consciousness. My jailers took me out of the water so I could come to. At the same time, they flogged my feet with a cord. My teeth were chattering so much they nearly broke.

'And now have you decided to talk?' their boss asked me.

My defenses not yet spent, I said nothing and was forcibly submerged once again in the water. The sensation of suffocating is horrible. I fought with such rage that I broke the binding attached to my feet. My fists were bleeding on the handcuffs. I was having an increasingly difficult time concentrating. This torture was repeated three or four more times.

'In your diary you have noted 2 p.m. With whom do you have a meeting?'

'With LeClercq', a made up name.

'Where?'

'At the Montparnasse train station.'

In reality, I had a rendezvous in the rue Littré at 4:30 p.m. and it risked nothing to lead them to the train station where I would perhaps have a chance to escape.

'Get dressed quickly.'

It was five minutes to two and they pushed me, wet and shivering, to try to make it in time for the meeting. Not realizing this was a fictitious meeting, the boss was upset.

'2:30 p.m. and he is still not here. If you are messing with us you will wind up back in the bathtub.'

'I can't do anything about it if he doesn't show up — he probably saw me in your car. You should have let me off on the sidewalk.'

We left for the rue des Saussaies to resume the nightmare of the "Bereitschaftzimmer", the shouts of the Gestapo, the groaning of their prisoners, the noises of locks and padlocks...

Time passed, heavily, oppressively. Will they force me to submit yet again to this horrible bathtub or would they find an even more atrocious torture? And the comrades with whom I had a meeting? Maxime and Personne, with whom I was supposed to meet for lunch, are they alerted, do they understand? I hope I don't break.

At 7 p.m. I was brought once again to bureau 533. The huge brute who tortured me proudly announced that the interrogation would resume the following day and threw me into the corridor. We were about fifteen people, noses to the wall, awaiting who knew what.

They made us go down to a huge room on the ground level where we found some forty odd males and females guarded by the "Boches", some in uniform and some in civilian clothing, armed with machine guns. It was there I found Jacques who had almost escaped.

He told me of his day: 'After having found in my datebook the list of meetings I had systematically noted one hour later than reality for security reasons, the Gestapo brought me to St. Germain-des-Prés to serve as bait. When I got to the middle of the square, I noticed the chain of my handcuffs was broken. I started running with all my might with them on my heels; they fired two dozen shots and missed. I was about to escape when a guy pushing a cart loaded with wood threw the cart in my path, tripping me up. Needless to say how the "Boches" brought me back here.'

We stayed in the huge room a long time before being transferred to Fresnes. In the prison courtyard, I found the concierge of the building where I had been arrested. He is a victim because of me, suspected of complicity. His wife had tried to warn me with her gaze ... I had not understood. The concierge did not hold it against me. I never saw him again or knew if he got out or was deported."

Thus Pierre was at Fresnes. He stayed forty-five days during which they told me he wasn't there. What was the purpose of this useless torture?

He was later transferred to Senlis, then to St. Quentin where he would experience the Gestapo's "boîtes", windowless closets, suffocating and dark, where prisoners were left from four to sixteen hours prior to interrogation under very intense lights, all with the purpose of breaking them. Pierre endured a fourteen hour session before being transferred again to Senlis, to a private property recently converted into a prison.

The rules for the "guests" at Senlis allowed for the receipt of packages, hence the mysterious messenger at the hôtel Edouard VII. The messenger was Robert who was, we would learn toward the end of the occupation, a liquor merchant. After D-day, he turned coat and came back to the French side, abandoning his boss, Dr. Schott. Because he had been helpful with the packages, we had him freed.

Having the chance to send Pierre a new package, I slipped in a note suggesting he pass his time by writing poetry for me. He understood immediately and sent me a harmless seeming verse that would not arouse anyone's suspicion. The first letter of the second word of each stanza spelled out the name of the place he was held. This personal code had allowed me to keep track of his whereabouts during the first part of the war. It was how I learned he was at Senlis and I was going to try to get him out. Feeling less scrutinized by the Gestapo, I reestablished contact with the Resistance network. That led me to maintain a small encoded address book for my clandestine meetings ...

SIX

FRANÇOISE
IN THE NAZI DUNGEON

On June 10, 1944 at 4 a.m., the doorbell rang, waking us with a start. The "Boches" told me this time that Pierre had escaped and that they were taking us all in, including the baby who was hardly more than a year old. The search of the apartment barely allowed me to hide some money in an old shoe and slip my address book behind a piece of furniture. It was not a good hiding place and I hoped it would just be temporary.

Despite my best efforts, our faithful Jeannine, who lived in the maid's room, was also arrested. Exchanging a few words with her, I realized she had had to turn over her keyring which held the key to the utility room where many compromising documents were hidden and bottles of Oliver's concentrated milk were also stored.

The car took us to a street near the avenue de la Grande Armée. They made us enter a dusty apartment and go into the dining room. There they placed Jeannine at one end of the room, face to the wall, and I was likewise placed at the other end.

The hours passed and the baby was getting fussy so I let him play. Our guard dozed. There were a lot of comings and goings in the apartment. Annette thought she spotted her aunt and I thought I had caught a glimpse of Farjon's (alias Dufor) wife. If true, that meant her husband had escaped with Pierre – they were together!

Taking advantage of the sleeping guard, I gave signals to the children whom I hoped would be freed before I was: "Get the address book and the key and make them disappear."

One of the Gestapo agents came to get me for a long three hour interrogation which turned into a political conversation. I took the opportunity to make a case for my daughters, arguing the point to which such an arrest of innocent children would incite hatred on the part of the French and propel to clandestine activities all those close to the arrested family. Not to mention the families of my children's schoolmates at Janson-de-Sailly High School. The students were all consolidated there when their original schools, Claude Bernard and La Fontaine, became German barracks.

Strangely, I found my interrogator shaken by my suggestion but I quickly realized it was a ploy to lead me into a trap. He seemed to accept my combativeness. With complicated digressions, he tried to get me to say what I knew about Pierre's past contacts and activities.

My adversary was not at all a brute and I felt completely capable of matching him mentally. On the other hand, how would I react to torture?

When the interrogation came to an end, he brought me to the

room where my sister-in-law, Mrs. Farjon and her mother-in-law were being held. The next stop for the four of us was prison ... but happily without Jeannine and the children who returned home, as I had requested in showing the damage it would do to the Germans. He had swallowed the bait.

The story of their return deserves to be told. The door to the apartment was opened by one of two soldiers ordered to keep an eye on Jeannine and the girls, particularly Annette. Barely inside the apartment, Florence, twelve years old, discreetly hurried to the living room to retrieve and hide the infamous address book.

It was an important accomplishment because one minute later the two Germans burst into the room. The balcony of the apartment was also being watched but that didn't prevent Florence from serving as a lookout in the hallway while Annette called from the kitchen window overlooking the interior courtyard to a fifth floor resident. The latter understood she was to call a neighbor friend. On and off, Florence sang a ditty that was a prearranged signal, and Annette and the resident were interrupted as soldiers entered the kitchen.

Finally the neighbor friend arrived. Still from the window, Annette explained what was happening, asking the neighbor friend to have the concierge station himself at the base of the building in the courtyard the kitchen looked out on. As soon as he appeared, she tossed the infamous key that so worried me and a note telling the concierges to prevent anyone, no matter whom, from phoning or coming to the apartment.

Two calls were mistakenly put through anyway and the Germans made Annette answer while they listened in on the extension. The first caller was a Resistance comrade, George, for whom I got a bicycle tire.

"I can't tell you anything, Mom has been arrested," Annette replied.

The Boches, furious, shoved her and demanded angrily "Who is this George – what's his real name?"

"I don't know. He's coming for the tire." Since the tire was there, the Germans didn't press the issue. The second call was from neighbors who wanted to give an update on Didier, who was at summer camp with their son. What they were really after was how they could help the children.

Throughout, these guys were searching everywhere and continued to question my daughters who knew to respond evasively. Since no call had come in from Pierre, who was luckily in an area temporarily without phone service, they finally left the apartment after three days.

Annette and Jeannine thus began the long treks to Fresnes, full of courage and laden with packages they tried to get delivered to Clotilde and me. They also made great efforts, similar to those they had seen me make on behalf of their father, while Jeannine cared for Olivier like a mother. Young and full of initiative, they never lost confidence in the future. Their laughter was testament to their confidence and vitality.

These same qualities were not lacking in their father, either, whose escape was no walk in the park as his story shows:

"I had been held for three weeks at Senlis in a building converted into a prison and where the German military security forces, evacuated from Arras following the bombings, were housed. My spirits were raised thanks to two packages I received via my captors.

Following an umpteenth sleepless night with my cellmate, Colonel Donnay, who was completely unhinged after being told he could write a final letter to his wife, I was taken to a guard post to be transferred to the fourth floor to a room with two beds, securely padlocked and with bars on the window. Farjon was already there, as dapper as usual.

We had barely been left alone when we spotted our path to escape. We were only about thirty feet off the ground. The solid wood door, having no peephole, prevented any surveillance from the outside; the guards could only get to our door by passing through another very noisy one. And only one watch of three guards patrolled the perimeter of the building. Having hatched his plan, Farjon had already gotten hold of a file and, after several hours of effort, we managed to loosen the seal around the bars. Bread crumbs mixed with mortar dust camouflaged our work. All we needed now was a rope. The two bedsheets torn lengthwise into strips would work perfectly. We decided to wait until midnight to act. When the time came, we removed the loosened bars, fastened the sheets and tied our shoes around our necks; we decided Farjon would go first. Though he scraped his palms sliding down the sheets and I hurt my wrist and lost my shoes falling the last ten feet, it didn't stop us from crossing the yard and scaling the wall surrounding the property.

When we got to the highway, we headed toward Compiègne, taking care to hide whenever a car approached. One of our priorities was to get to a telephone to alert our families of the escape so they could try to avoid arrest. My wrist was killing me and the loss of my shoes posed a real problem.

There was no village before Verberie which we had decided not to go through, fearing German sentries. We went around it, going over fences and barbed wire, and got back on the road to Compiègne. The trip became difficult, walking in a driving rain with bloodied feet and a painful wrist.

At six in the morning, we got to Croix-Saint-Ouen, a small village where Farjon knew the manager of a factory owned by his relatives, a man who would welcome us as friends. Finally we would be able to alert our families. But telephone service in the Oise area was cut off from the rest of the country. I would later learn that my family had already been arrested at four a.m.

After being fed and having my wrist bandaged, we left at about nine a.m. toward Paris. We made the journey hidden under large sacks of coal in a big box on the back of one of the factory trucks. Farjon's friend himself drove us, assisted by two chauffeurs. We avoided Senlis by going through Creil and Chantilly. We arrived in Paris close to noon and each of us set out in search of a place to hide.

I quickly found a safe house where I stayed just long enough to eat, clean up, and have a surgeon come to set my broken wrist. The search for a good hideout was challenging. I stayed in a succession of places including at an ophthalmologist's home, a maid's quarters and with several old friends before I began to feel a bit safe.

I made contact with what remained of my group. I just barely missed being taken again when I received word after the fact of a meeting set for July 28, 1944 with Rondenay, alias Jerry, who was arrested that very morning. I later learned he was going to give me a new assignment. Arrested less than a month before Liberation, the poor soul was gunned down near Paris after having been taken prisoner of war, escaped, then made head of the BCRA, (Bureau Central de Renseignement et d'Action), de Gaulle's main agency of governing the Résistance, for the northern zone."

While Pierre was on the run with Farjon, I was transferred to Fresnes, escorted by the secretary of the head of the Gestapo who told me my husband had erred in escaping with Farjon who worked for the Germans and had betrayed his comrades. Why would he tell me that? "You will tell his wife", he added without another word.

My arrival at Fresnes marked the beginning of a long episode which would last six weeks and which I will never forget. Stripped of all my personal belongings, including the belt from my dress, I was led to a cell with no water. There was nothing but a bed with a straw mattress and two blankets. The walls were covered with various messages telling of the uneasiness, boredom and hopelessness of the women who had been locked up here before me.

I readied myself for my first night in prison. I heard mysterious taps from time to time. I would later understand their meaning.

The next day at dawn, the door to my cell was opened abruptly. I found myself among other prisoners who had also been arrested the previous day. Before being directed to our permanent cells, we exchanged a few words. One of the women had been submerged seven times and beaten. Her face and body black and blue from the blows, she was proud she had not talked and said, despite her sad face, "Take courage, be happy." Instinctively I gave her the sugar Annette had stealthily slipped to me when I was arrested. I would go without, but I would not regret it. By contrast, a plump Austrian woman timidly asked me "What are they going to do to us?"

A poor old peasant woman was there, calm and saying little, and others, too.

After almost sharing a cell for two, I wound up alone and preferred it that way. Sure, being able to talk would pass the time, but the lack of fresh air, space to move around and privacy was worse. I was not unhappy to be left alone with photos of my family. But soon the minutes turned to hours and the hours to days. And I would soon know the suffering of hunger.

About every ten days we were permitted to walk for ten minutes but forbidden to signal to anyone we met along the way. Despite this measure, communication between prisoners happened as soon as the cart arrived to distribute bread and soup because the noise of the wheels covered up the sound of voices. The water pipes also permitted communication between adjacent cells.

The challenge was not getting caught. The punishment for the offense was being thrown immediately into the dungeon.

Condemned to death and held incommunicado for a year, the woman in the adjacent cell had moments of utter despair. She could no longer bear being locked up, unable to move about and with no word of her family. Her mother died of the aftereffects of an interrogation shortly before her own arrest. She knew nothing else. All she had left was a sister suffering from tuberculosis, with a sickly five year old child and a husband who was a POW in Germany. This staunch Communist was tenderhearted. Through the water pipe she told me about her mother:

"She was still so young and pretty and she loved us so. A lowly seamstress, a humble worker, she dressed us with such taste and elegance that her clients wanted the same outfits we had."

My other neighbor, Susy, was a postman's wife. She had a fourteen year old son. Arrested as an accomplice of her brother-in-law, she had been told she would be deported to Germany. "I've been here three months. Does my family even know that I am here?"

Another inmate, Jeannette, called desperately each morning for Jeannot who did not answer. He forged papers for forced labor objectors and Resistance fighters. She was a sales clerk in a small lingerie boutique. The militia had come to arrest them. Everyone at Fresnes, over and above the boredom, worried about their loved ones without any way of knowing what was going on outside.

Generally, new arrivals had no right to packages, from family or the Red Cross, until the end of the first month. But that was really arbitrary. Arrested the same day and on the same grounds, the mother and wife of Pierre's partner in the escape and my sister-in-law and I would not receive the same treatment. We were all held in isolation except Farjon's wife. Some would receive packages right away, others much later, but never the same number of packages over the same time period. The number of interrogations would vary as would the duration of punishments and the granting of small privileges: for example, getting a bar of soap or a toothbrush or books.

In addition to the problems of isolation and inactivity, there was hunger. It wasn't noticeable at first, probably due to the lack of fresh air and the stress. Theoretically, our one daily meal consisted of a piece of black bread and cabbage soup with beans or noodles served in a rusty metal bowl, but in reality it looked and tasted like dishwater. I only once found a single bean in the broth. My first package from the Red Cross didn't arrive until the sixth week.

Not wishing to drink the bromide-laced black water that was served in the place of coffee and made me vomit – in order to keep a clear head for the interrogations – I was unable to sleep and suffered the assault each night of fleas and lice which I couldn't fend off in the dark.

About every three weeks, the pleasure of being able to shower was willfully spoiled by the guards. They turned the water on and off without warning, leaving us, at their whim, from one to ten minutes to wash. Since the shower doors were abruptly opened to allow the Boches to enjoy the show, it frequently occurred that we would already be dressed only to be drenched when they turned the water on again.

Although it was forbidden, I was obsessed with cracking the window to get a breath of fresh air and some sun. This would, on one occasion, get me three days in the dungeon without food. My only pastime was to read the messages on the walls from those who had previously suffered there. And I added my own with pieces of broken plaster since sleep was impossible without bed, mattress or even a blanket. I had only a three legged chair and, not wanting to get dirty, I used it. Keeping my balance on it exhausted me.

Suffering from cold and lack of food, I was suddenly suffocating and my teeth began to chatter. My nose was clogged and my limbs began to jerk. I heard a harsh cry beside me:

"Get up!"

A guard had entered. She took my pulse, then left. I started to come to as they brought me some hot soup. Little by little, I came back to life.

The return to my cell was practically cause for celebration. My neighbors had kind words for me. And I was so happy to get back to my blanket, my bed and my meager pittance! And I rejoined my network of prisoners who would, in the evenings near their windows, exchange war news. With poor communication through the walls, passed from section to section, the news was also embellished by the imagination of the detainees. "Rouen bombed" became "Rouen liberated".

Also, about every eight days, there was an interrogation which, for me, took place at Fresnes rather than rue des Saussaies or avenue Foch or elsewhere.

Schott, my German adversary, was intelligent and more sly than rough. Rather heavy and bald, he tried to win my confidence. He also bragged that he was more effective than the brutes who had tortured Pierre. On leaving prison I would learn he was not wrong. If Resistance prisoners endured the torture, they had a harder time getting through two hours with this sly fox, so well informed by the traitor among them.

He spoke to me right away about the infamous Farjon whom the Gestapo chief's secretary had already named. I took the information with a grain of salt, coming as it did from a German.

Diving into the game, he laid out evidence and tried to get me to recognize other names, all the while claiming to already know them. He put a list of 157 people in front of me, of whom 80 were, according to him, already arrested. I held fast to my previous statements:

"I know nothing of my husband's real or imagined activities and know none of these names."

One fine day my opponent said: "It's futile to deny it, I know you are aware of your husband's activities but I won't tell anyone. I will look into getting you out of here." The trap was crude.

"Well if you know, why ask me? What proof do you have?"

"All the Resistance fighters' wives are aware of their husband's activities."

"Then I am the exception."

Probably wanting to bring up the fact that I am Jewish, he added that he had another charge against me…

"Tell me what it is and show me the proof."

My show of confidence made him lose his. I began to sense he doubted my complicity with Pierre. My adversary left me in peace for three weeks.

During this period, the battle of Normandy was continuing without significant progress. Behind our prison bars we managed nonetheless to glean some information and waited for a swift advance of the Anglo-Saxon troops toward Paris.

On one morning as sad as all the others, I was called one more time to the tribunal to learn from my adversary of my release as well as that of my sister-in-law and the two Farjon women.

"Do you confirm your statements about M. Farjon?"

"It's no longer the moment to speak of that."

And so I had to leave my cell neighbors, and to learn by heart the maximum number of addresses so I could deliver news of the detainees to their families, and to reunite with Clotilde with whom I had had no communication these many long weeks.

Rejoining the Farjon women, I sadly thought of what was in store for them. They were so happy at the idea of regaining their freedom and especially of seeing their loved one whom they thought a hero. In the face of such pure love, a doubt persisted in my mind.

Convinced we were being released to lure the escapees from their hiding places, Clo and I decided to be very careful. The return we so looked forward to did not match our hopes. Clo's place had been burglarized and my children had left eight days earlier to stay at the home of friends in Bures-sur-Yvettes in the Chevreuse valley.

My first taste of bread with butter and sugar, offered on first sight of us by a generous neighborhood grocer, was like rediscovering paradise. And the two days of waiting to see Annette, Florence and baby Olivier were quickly forgotten. Didier was still at the summer camp, taken with other children from the St.Jeanne de Chantal parish by the curate, who feared a long siege of the capital like the one in 1870.

My sister-in-law and I did not forget to take the many messages to the families of our cell neighbors still detained.

As for Pierre, that was still a mystery, but I was confident. And news was good – the Americans had broken through the front and were preparing to march into Paris.

In August 1944, little by little, people let their guards down. Paris fought, Paris was in open insurgency. Though we were living through glorious hours, full of hope despite the noise of cannons and machine guns, our joy was turned to grief by a phone call.

The husband of a Jewish cousin, Dr. Frankel, whose family had not fled Paris despite the risk of deportation, told me that his young son, Biqui, age seventeen and a half, had just been fatally wounded, having wanted to take part in the liberation of Paris. Before he died, he told his parents that Jacques, his elder brother who was a POW in Germany, would be proud to learn he had succeeded in disarming Germans and killing two of them. Idealistic and passionate, this intelligent and studious young man, who had just passed his baccalaureate with distinction, had mailed a letter to his parents before leaving to complete "his" mission. They received it after he died …

"Dear parents,

Forgive me for having disobeyed you and forgive me for any pain I may cause you. I am leaving to carry out a mission. It is my duty …"

The unfortunate child was buried the same morning that General Leclerc's tanks arrived. And Clotilde, Annette and I made our way across Paris on bicycle, in mourning dress, to attend the religious service.

On our way back, we encountered the victors, cheered by crowds, when, suddenly, machine gun fire erupted from the roofs of buildings and windows. The soldiers quickly remounted their turrets and returned fire while the crowd didn't know where to seek cover.

A few days later, Pierre came home. We had so many things to tell each other. But the reunion was brief. Sent on a mission by de Gaulle, he left Paris in August just before the Liberation was complete. His objective was significant: get to the St. Quentin region and install new leaders, secretly appointed by de Gaulle, in the four prefectures of the Aisne, Ardennes, Oise and Somme. He would also welcome the Anglo-Saxon troops and represent, as Regional Commissaire, the GPRF (Gouvernement Provisoire de la République Française) to the Allies.

He would also go on to reestablish communications and supplies for the region, prepare for the return of deportees, and make ready for new elections.

The installation of de Gaulle loyalists, who replaced préfets of the Vichy regime, went pretty smoothly. The FFI (Forces Françaises de l'Intérieur) pulled together the various clandestine military Resistance groups and actively participated with the Allies and the FFL (Forces Françaises Libres) in freeing French territory until the signing of the Armistice in May 1945. The fighting resulted in many casualties. There were acts of heroism by a large number of young men, anxious to fight face to face an enemy they had only been able to slyly resist during the long years of occupation.

After this time of heroism for some and pain for most, hope returned. And a disappointing peace accompanied the corteges of the near dead returning from the Nazi camps with their horrific stories. And there were betrayals coming to light.

The name Farjon, alias Dufor, came up again. Why had death not claimed him when he was fighting during the Liberation on the Alsatian front and wounded twice? Mystery of fate.

An OCM complaint was filed so there was a trial. Pierre and I were called to testify. Before being killed in a tragic car accident, our friend Lepercq, Farjon's brother-in-law, who was at Fresnes at the same time as I, and who was appointed Finance Minister at Liberation, asked us, not in so many words, to point out the traitor. He was reluctant because of his family ties which the writer Gilles Perrault called "the ghetto of resistance of the sixteenth arrondissement" in a book about the OCM, "The Long Hunt".

Pierre would be named a "Compagnon de la Libération", a great honor. I would receive the Medal of the Resistance, presented to me by General Koenig at Baden-Baden before a small battalion.

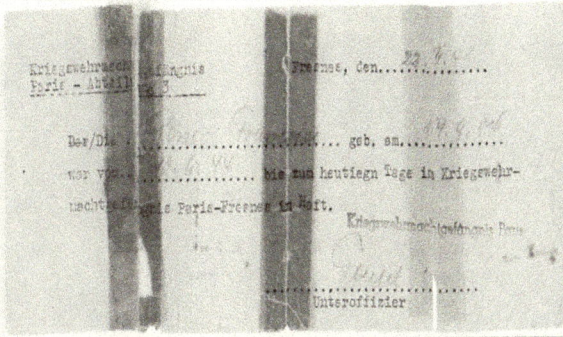

Release ticket for Françoise

General Koenig awarding the Resistance Medal
to Françoise Pène in August 1945

Pierre Pène, at General de Gaulle's left, in Beauvais, August 11, 1945. Also present: three ministers, the Préfet de l'Oise, and military officials.

SEVEN

PIERRE, "COMMISSAIRE DE LA RÉPUBLIQUE"

Our stay in St. Quentin at war's end, full of hope and confusion, was not without interest.

My first priority was getting Didier from the summer camp where the curate of St. Jeanne de Chantal parish had taken him and a group of other young boys from Paris and Boulogne. Pierre's chauffeur took me and I finally located Didier hidden away at a nearby farm. The summer camp directors had thought it best to put him there as a precaution, following a suspicious visit concerning the Pène family. It turned out not to be the Germans but rather Pierre's friends surreptitiously checking on him.

Didier was in bad shape, filthy and covered in pimples. Nine years old at the end of the war, he thought he had been abandoned because his sisters had foolishly concealed my arrest. Albeit they had been prohibited from telling him the truth, their evasive answers upset him even more, on top of the fact he thought his father was dead. The priests simply told him to pray for him...

Back in St. Quentin, I took him to the doctor who diagnosed an exposure to TB. Proper care rapidly brought him back into shape. But this period during which he received evasive explanations, which caused him to feel rejected by his family, would have after-effects for many years to come. I would only notice them as he entered adolescence...

Quickly settled in our official villa at the beginning of autumn 1944, I hurried to prepare for the return of those who had been deported (i.e. returning from concentration, work and prisoner of war camps), to locate funds to create a welcome center and to maintain a rest home to help the families.

To support that, I organized some shows and fairs which raised significant money, mostly from industrialists and real estate moguls who seized the opportunity to wipe the slate clean of any misconduct related to the black market or collaboration with the Nazis. And the success with the various political parties was remarkable – they wanted to use these events for political propaganda. Out of twenty booths, the communists demanded nine and kept nine/tenths of the proceeds for the Party.

Having admired the courage of my neighbor cellmate at Fresnes, the pure and steadfast communist condemned to death, I was quickly disgusted by their constant schemes, for example, distributing surplus food ration coupons only to card-carrying members of the Party! Or the way they delighted in taking the proceeds, basically making their electoral stake on the backs of these poor wretches. I lodged a complaint, seconded by the "préfet" whom I had alerted, against the "sous-préfet" who was very lax about these goings-on. The MRP (Mouvement Républicain Populaire) and the Socialists followed suit with the Communist practices in trying to grab the loot. I left it in the hands of the social aid workers who were neutral.

My mother had taken refuge at Cap-d'Ail during the

occupation but, upon Liberation, came to live with Annette in the rue de la Tourelle in Boulogne. Always passionate about classical music, she retained a youthful appearance despite the privations. Her regular visits to St. Quentin brought me back to my adolescence when she lived as she wished and took no interest in material things.

As soon as she was settled in with us, my mother recreated her bohemian world, ignoring my social obligations as both hostess and wife of a highly placed civil servant. Her son, coming to visit us, behaved likewise. My mother was as indulgent as ever of my brother, Alain, at the time thirty-eight, from whom she put up with anything, including his taking whatever she owned, which allowed his participation in dubious schemes. A week after leaving me, she had an attack that left her in a coma for several days before she passed away at age sixty-eight.

Her passing profoundly affected me, even though I had been so little troubled by my father's death when I was eleven; he had always been so remote. Long afterward, I would notice how, as we approached the age of their deaths, the departed one would seem to come back to life in the form of our physical traits or in our children's behavior.

Nonetheless, my grief dissipated quickly, overwhelmed as I was with all the needs and tasks that confronted me.

For his part, Pierre, representing de Gaulle's government, faced many difficulties, the first of which was military in nature. In December 1944, von Rundstedt's last ditch attack, a wildcat stampede in the Ardennes, required Pierre to make some extremely difficult decisions in the absence of orders from the Ministry of the Interior. Even though weather conditions prevented any support from their air force, the Americans at Bastogne refused to give up. Pierre closed the border to reassure the panicked Ardennais. He made every effort to keep the roads

clear so American tanks could get through. It was for naught.
Tension mounted for several days when finally, on Christmas Eve,
the skies cleared, allowing the planes to take off and free the
trapped Allies, half of whom had frozen feet. I would later come
to know one of these young guys, who would become my son-in-
law!

There were major problems in the civilian population as well.
Following the systematic pillaging by the Germans, the region
needed everything. There were no trains or bridges, and the roads
were highly damaged. Food supplies were exhausted. Added to
these problems was the lack of a police force, largely decimated
with the fall of the Vichy government. Not to mention the
Communists who were bent on taking power. My neighbor
cellmate at Fresnes had talked about that at the beginning of 1944.

When Hitler attacked the Soviet Union, the French
Communists mobilized to secretly fight the Nazis with great
courage and in the name of revolution, but they did not act out of
the same spirit as the patriots. Their goal was not to free the
country but to take it over.

Other civil disturbances, such as the excessive vengeance –
often understandable– against those who had denounced Jews or
Resistance fighters, severely upset law and order.

Pierre successfully overcame so many such obstacles. His role
as Commissaire of the Republic was of short duration. Pressured
by the dual attack by the opposition parties, the MRP and the
Communists, the eighteen "Commissariats" were abolished and
the prefectures restored to authority. Pierre considered running in
the soon-to-be-held Senate elections.

Finally he was named Governor of Baden in 1946. It was one of
the most brilliant assignments of his career and one of the most
interesting periods of our lives.

Pierre Pène and General Koenig at Fribourg in 1946

Françoise and General Koenig at Umkirch Chateau – the Pène family's residence – in 1949. Photo by Cr. Genzlers (photographer no longer determinable).

EIGHT

PIERRE –
GOVERNOR OF THE
GERMAN STATE OF BADEN

Gone alone to Freiburg im Breisgau to evaluate the "kolossal" task ahead of him, Pierre, the new Governor of Baden, sent for me and Annette to join him several days later ... We arrived by train in Strasbourg where Pierre's chauffeur was waiting for us in a pretty burgundy torpedo car. He gave us a tour of the town before getting on the road. How could we resist the temptation of a gastronomic shopping trip after so many years of deprivation? The beautiful season obliged us and we indulged our preference for marvelous red fruit and filled the trunk of the convertible with them.

A few kilometers after crossing the border, we had a flat and had to stop in the open with no shade while the tire was changed. It was a chance to taste our fruit on the side of the road. We were wind-blown and our hands were stained red from the juice when we were surprised by an exceptionally loud horn.

Intrigued by this official cortege preceded by motorcycles and an officer standing in a small car ready to clear the road, if necessary, we watched an enormous Mercedes pass, followed by another car. I learned later that the Mercedes was formerly Hitler's car.

The vehicle at the end did a half-turn and came toward us. On the running board, a tall young man offered us his help and told us, in response to my query, the name of the official being transported in the cortege ... It was none other than Pierre. The prestigious future, full of obligations for the Governor and the Pène family, was upon us.

Two days later, leaving Mercystrasse with Florence, Didier and little Olivier who had joined us, we headed to visit the medieval section of Freibourg im Breisgau and its pink sandstone cathedral whose pointed and filigreed steeple rose nobly in the midst of the ruins of buildings destroyed by Nazi bombs —and I do mean Nazi— in German territory . It was the Corpus Christi feast day and the grounds of the plaza and adjacent roads were decorated with flowers. The windows of neighboring homes were trimmed with old tapestries and brocaded silk. Inside the cathedral, the devout congregation sang. Olivier, a beautiful baby with blond curls, made clear he wanted to see more of what was going on and several people offered to hoist him above the crowd. This kindness made an impression on me as we were obviously the "occupying French". It taught me right away to distinguish between the Germans and the Nazis, the latter particularly disliked in the Baden region where Hitler didn't dare come even in his heyday.

It's a distinction our allies would have a hard time grasping whereas General de Gaulle had no hesitation in meeting Chancellor Adenauer, a Christian Democrat. Pierre would likewise work on Franco-German rapprochement when he organized the Constance Conference in 1949.

Built on the side of a mountain, the charming villa we took on arrival was insufficient for the various receptions coming up.

People from around the world wanted to visit and understand the vanquished country whose devastated people had made such trouble for the world.

Pierre's chief of staff, trying his best, showed me over-decorated homes of dubious taste. After many fruitless efforts, I went without much hope to visit a mosquito-infested chateau about five miles from town, and I fell in love with it at first sight for its architectural elegance, harmonious proportions and pink hue. It was situated in a charming open space with a magnificent pond.

Learning that the chateau had belonged to Stephanie de Beauharnais, (Napoleon's adopted daughter, married to the Duke of Baden), I found the following information about the period in Françoise de Bernardy's book:

"On August 11, 1827, the Duchess left for Umkirch which she and her daughters returned to with pleasure..."

A description by the Duchess's daughter, Josephine, followed:

"We are now at Umkirch, a very pretty property belonging to my mother, near Freibourg. There's an extremely pretty Italian-style chateau in a large garden with a park. We enjoy it even more because there is also a lake with a small island in the garden."

The present owner of the property, Prince Frederic of Hohenzollern, was hoping to cohabit with some French official so as to get the chateau heated. Even though he was obligated to cooperate, he gladly accepted the rent we proposed and to move to a secondary villa not far from the chateau. The Prince's wife, a woman of character, sought to associate with us. We held back a bit, especially me. Like her grandmother who ran off with a musician, she pursued Pierre and quickly emptied her glasses of liquor. On the other hand, she was an excellent musician, and pleasant.

Umkirch Chateau

For the umpteenth time, but always with the same enthusiasm, I organized our new home, regrouping the furniture according to style. I uncovered rickety riches in the attic and basement which I had quickly restored by a local cabinetmaker. I also ordered some less fragile furniture to redo the princess's apartment as we had allowed her to take her things out to the smaller villa. I had some chairs made to round out the number of existing ones, quite beautiful, but insufficient in number for the double-sized dining room. I also sought out porcelain-makers of dishware and accessories who had withdrawn their wares from the market because they did not want to be paid with devalued marks.

Town gardeners removed the poppy field, a vestige of a time when skinny cows were grazed there, and planted grass on the lawn. They replanted flowers in abundance. Four days after my arrival at Umkirch, I prepared to host General Koenig for Pierre's swearing-in ceremony.

The first big dinner for fifty-four was a complete success and I hit it off immediately with General Koenig, the hero of Bir Hakeim, who told me in all modesty "Not being titled and not graduating from a prestigious school, I would only be a captain had it not been for the war"!

Our second big reception was to bring together all the French expatriates and we had a huge ball with two orchestras. An enormous dance floor was installed behind the chateau, with lighting to emphasize the pink stone and the XVIIIth century architecture.

For six years we led a very fashionable, worldly existence, alternating among cocktail parties, official dinners, children's teas, Christmas parties as well as invitations we could not turn down.

Among the numerous guests of all nationalities from all corners of the globe whom we welcomed at Umkirch, two would turn out to be particularly disagreeable.

The first was an important English socialist, whose name I have forgotten, who accused the French under Napoleon of having been as aggressive as the Nazis! The second would become very well known – it was Francois Mitterrand, then Minister of Prisoners and Veterans. Already in 1945, he acted like a little monarch. He arrived with his staff director and Alain Poher; the latter was always very well-mannered and invited us later to visit Rhineland.

We put them up in our three guest suites. The rest of Mitterrand's entourage would be housed, for better or worse, by Pierre's chief of staff in a guest house in Freibourg, five miles from the chateau.

Informed of the lodging arrangements, Mitterrand, domineering and shameless, insisted that his very private secretary be housed under the same roof as he:

"Make it happen" he told me pretentiously, as I tried to explain there were no other free rooms in the chateau.

Not wanting to make a scene, I sent Annette to sleep in the maid's room at a friend's house in town. But the redoubtable Mitterrand didn't let it go at that. He also ordered me to get perfume for his wife, categorically refusing once again to recognize the supply difficulties of this postwar period.

His conceit shocked me, as did the order he made me place at the commissary for items in excess of the rations, especially since I held my family and Pierre's aides to the strictest conformance with the rules.

This life, tiring but fascinating at the same time, was shared by the entire family. Annette, petite, lively, pretty and dynamic with a graceful décolleté, looked ravishing in evening gowns and elicited great compliments. Florence, five years her junior, was a high school student and then a psychology major in Strasbourg. Hers was a more sculptured beauty and was very intelligent; she equally charmed my guests. Didier, in high school, considered these social events drudgery to be avoided. And very young and handsome Olivier attended a nun's kindergarten at the beginning of our stay and then the village school, before attending, at age seven, the French elementary school in Fribourg. He made my German guests laugh with his local Baden accent and often served as my interpreter.

Pierre Pène and General Koenig in 1948

Our attire preoccupied us quite a bit. I hired a dressmaker and had her copy variations, mostly in fabric, of the dresses modeled and sold at design houses I knew. I also had her make dresses of my own design for my daughters and me.

Never had my role as lady of the house been more important than at Umkirch where I had to oversee everything: the decor, naturally, but also the menus which required great care to ensure that I offered delicious meals while staying within my budget. That led me to compare prices between Alsace and Baden, especially for wine, and to go to Basel in Switzerland for more rare foodstuffs.

I also had to oversee table seating arrangements prepared by Pierre's chief of staff. They entailed strict protocols which did not take into account the languages or interests of our guests.

In France, wives of officials have at their disposal a well selected and competent staff. That was not the case at Umkirch where a so-called Romanian prince, a very imaginative snob, poorly recruited the household staff. For example, he made me hire a junior officer who had worked for General Schwartz, Pierre's predecessor; he shamelessly stole from me from the start. His technique consisted of noting with great detail the prices of items purchased from the commissary, then adding offhanded round sums of 300 to 500 marks under a generic category. With moving expenses and the cost of the balls, I didn't notice the overcharges right away...

I'd have better luck with the next two, a junior reserve officer and a father of a family, respectively, whom I hired myself.

A bit later, the would-be Romanian prince carefully proposed a governess to oversee the staff and give German lessons to Olivier. I let myself be talked into it as I didn't know the country or the staff well. But this woman displeased me immediately. I felt her to be indoctrinated with Nazism. She suggested I buy a sack of leather tanned by her father as an exchange for hard-to-find foodstuffs such as coffee. I showed her the door!

I had stayed in touch with Marie-Rose, a former maid in Soissons who had recently divorced. She was mother of a five year old little girl. I decided to have her stay with us, convinced she would be a good governess since she would be raising her own child at our expense. I moved them both into the best room with a flower-filled terrace on the third floor.

Marie-Rose was not hired to clean. Her work consisted of passing on my orders and personally distributing the precious foodstuffs to the staff to avoid the more than 10% shrinkage we had been experiencing.

Unfortunately, this solution was not perfect. She was not the right class for this role of steward nor did she speak German. Her hair was unkempt and she was too plump. Her daughter totally lacked discretion and constantly barged in on our gatherings.

At the same time, I felt indulgent toward this employee who had left for Cier during the evacuation of 1940 with my mother-in-law and my three children who were so attached to her.

Like the role of steward, responsible for purchasing and food management, the role of housekeeper is indispensable to a well-managed household. She must ensure the direct oversight of the three chambermaids, a butler, three gardeners and a cook and his assistant! Besides my small family and house staff, we also had to feed the guards, the head of the carpool and his three chauffeurs. That made a total of twenty-eight people to feed each day. Add to that the six hundred meals per month for official luncheons and dinners, not to mention the major receptions, cocktail parties, balls and garden parties.

Under the cook's authority fell the preparation of meals in a villa fifty yards from the chateau, equipped with a "kolossal" kitchen and cold room for storing large cuts of meat. The talent of our master cook, an excellent chef and baker, able to meet schedules, estimate quantities, and maintain a clean kitchen, caused me to accept his stubborn refusal to work at the chateau when we didn't have a lot of guests.

Regularly inventorying the wine cellar with the steward, I realized expensive wines and liquors were disappearing. A discreet investigation began of the few people who held the keys. My steward suspected Marie-Rose who was, according to him, seeing a German chauffeur. He warned me not to trust her. Knowing her since she was sixteen, I couldn't come to grips with his suspicions. Following another theft, the cook's young assistant confessed and promised not to do it again. The matter was considered closed.

Some time later, I got double pneumonia that kept me in bed

for several weeks and I entrusted Marie-Rose with the key to the desk that contained money. I decided to follow the doctor's advice and convalesce in the Midi in France.

A few days before leaving, strolling in the park to get some air, I came across Françoise, Marie-Rose's daughter, suffering a slight cold and not warmly dressed. Her mother had the day off to go to Alsace to buy, I later learned, presents for her lover, so I accompanied her daughter to her room to get a sweater. Seeing an open parcel addressed to Marie-Rose's parents and, knowing how dizzy she was, I verified that she had included some small items I had given her for a young nephew. Instead, I was stupefied to discover unopened boxes of cigars, cigarettes, an embroidered outfit lent by a cousin, and other trinkets belonging to me, well packed in the carton.

Confronting her in my office when she returned, I uncovered the plot. A veritable network was at work in the house and the cook's young assistant, in reality innocent, had been pushed by the others into confessing to throw off the scent.

Astounded by such ingratitude, I sent Marie-Rose packing, choosing not to have her arrested but advising her to leave the country right away or I would have her deported and reported to her parents. Ultimately, it came to that. Instead of leaving, she thought it was better to move into town with her lover who would turn out to be a real pimp!

Tongues loosened and I learned that, for example, during my illness, Marie-Rose had had the dressmaker make things for her and her daughter using rare fabrics we had gotten under the rationing quotas.

After this episode, the village peasants of Umkirch would thereafter use the name Marie-Rose to designate a thief. And to think that we had gone to great lengths to show the people of Baden that the French were really not as Nazi propaganda would suggest!

Marie-Rose's departure seemed to mark the end of the thefts. But I remained careful, finding certain small things strange. I always planned for two river trout per person but there was never enough for everyone to have a second serving, and half empty bottles of wine were never seen again. I learned much later from the major-domo of the hôtel de Paris in Monte Carlo that this kind of pilfering happens around the world.

One day, after doing a few laps in the pool, I suddenly started sneezing and got up to get a handkerchief from my room. When I reached our suite, I saw a new servant turn around, visibly shaken by my presence. I then saw the butler, a German baron, there to fix a pipe in the bathroom, so he said. Of course it didn't really need it. Looking closely at my desk where I kept money and jewelry, I noticed fresh scratch marks around the lock. This time, Pierre and I called the French police who investigated and identified the guilty parties. Marie-Rose's gang had reconstituted itself quickly and the young newcomer was hired to be the lookout. The young woman was sent away and the German baron received three months in prison, firm despite his mother's appeal to Pierre for mercy…"This condemnation will leave a stain on our coat of arms", she pleaded in vain. Little Olivier, with a three year old's instincts, had always called him "the devil".

The new butler ascended the stairs barefoot to catch unawares the eldest, Annette, too carefree, in her underwear. The next, a professional, liked the bottle too much and would serve himself at mealtime.

After his departure, tongues once again loosened and a servant showed the steward the hiding place in the wall where the butler quickly stored the half-filled bottles and other leftovers from the table, right under the steward's nose. He not only fed his wife and mistress but maybe his mother as well. He must have been selling on the black market, too. I decided to take direct control of the personnel.

The next butler was a German who had served in the French Foreign Legion; he was rather stupid and salacious and, to our every interaction, would reply "I who died for France". At fifty years old, he ran away with his eighteen year old stepdaughter.

Despite the bad experience, I engaged a legionnaire working as a guard, originally from Danzig. A good-looking boy, refined and pleasant, Alfred managed well and was assisted by the head maid, a plump blonde, who was smitten with him and soon became pregnant. Hiding her pregnancy from me by cinching her waist, she suffered a terrible pain and unfortunately gave birth to a handicapped child. Alfred, who wasn't from the local village and had no money, had to wait two years, the time it took him to buy furniture, to marry Hilde and gain her family's acceptance.

When we arrived there, the local population seemed docile and apathetic. After the Hitlerian mirage, the defeat seemed to them to be inexplicable and unjust. The people refused to open their eyes to the regime's horrors and didn't accept their own responsibility for supporting the Führer and his ideology – racist, domineering and expansionist. All the while projecting their antinazi sentiments, the people of Baden refused to go see exhibits about the atrocities in the camps, arguing that all that was falsified.

Our contacts with the locals were, under orders from Paris, reserved, that is to say only official in nature. The allied Governors had to select a President for each "Land" or state. Pierre chose for his area a well-known anti-Nazi, Mr. Wohleb. Short, stocky and unattractive, this literature professor was cultured, honest and a fine diplomat. Later, when the vanquished population was permitted to select its own leader, he would be reconfirmed in the post until the areas of Baden and Württemberg were merged in 1952. Having expressed his opposition to the unification, he was posted as Ambassador to Portugal.

Françoise with (left to right) Robert Schuman, Minister of Foreign Affairs who contributed to founding the European Union, Bishop Robert Picard de la Vacquerie, André François-Poncet, High Commissioner of the French Occupied Zone in Germany, and Dr. Wohleb, President of Baden, 1949.

The policy of the western allies – American, English and French – was aimed at removing any thought of German revenge. All the same, their techniques varied. France, for example, sought to restore German morale in order to stabilize Europe. The objective was to replace central power with a federation of provinces with budgets partially independent of Bonn, with a view to creating a balance in Europe united with Holland, Luxembourg, Belgium and Italy, as well as a less severe severance from the east. Pierre was seeking means to achieve this but Great Britain, still seeking to maintain its own dominance by dividing Europe, thwarted his plans.

Poorly understanding the objectives of these small nations, the Americans wanted above all else to avoid a financial catastrophe like the one in the U.S. in 1929 or the one that brought Hitler to power in 1933.They also wanted to block the Communists and, in 1947, proposed the Marshall Plan for Reconstruction for sixteen European nations. It was adopted in 1948. There were also periods of extreme tension between East and West as demonstrated most notably by the Berlin blockade in June 1948 followed by the erection of the Berlin Wall in 1961. The wall would not come down until 1989.

During this postwar period, the Germans worked with determination and courage despite the major devaluation of the mark imposed by the Allies. France, by contrast, was suffering a crisis of political instability aggravated by the unraveling of its colonies.

Pierre owed his allegiance to General Koenig, the Commander in Chief of the French Occupied Zone until 1949 when Ambassador François Poncet took over. The two men, so very different, were much admired. The former, a globetrotting adventurer, courageous, dynamic, and intelligent was immediately likeable despite his maddening tendency to like a little too much the barracks humor of the enlisted men. I found him amusing and we had fun together. On my first visit to Berlin, I was accompanied by the Belgian Ambassador and Baroness Guillaume who had come to attend the medal ceremony for Belgian soldiers who were staying in the French sector of the former German capital. Having mentioned my desire to see Berlin, I was invited by my frequent dinner partner, the likeable hero of Bir Hakeim (French troops commanded by General Koenig stopped the Germans and Italians for 16 days allowing the British Army to mobilize and triumph at El Alamein), to take advantage of the availability of his personal plane. The ceremony ended with a ball given by General Koenig and was remarkable for the skills of the dancers and the mood set by our host. I wore a bespoke dress, hand-painted by a German artist, in fiery red, white and black on a green background and cut, per my direction, with a large skirt, a cinched waist and a charming low-cut bodice. The General, whose wife was the most elegant woman in Germany, complimented me all the same.

The next day, the General suggested we visit the city but cautioned us to avoid any transactions with antique dealers. We would understand this caution better from the police officer who served as our guide. His subordinates, for example, who earned five thousand francs per month, were entitled to two and a half a pound of coffee which the Germans begged them to sell for ten thousand francs per half pound. It was similar with the antique dealers where the officers of the four occupying forces could get beautiful jewelry, silver, Bohemian crystal and the like for just a few packs of cigarettes.

Our visit took us to the infamous chancellery where Hitler and Goebbels committed suicide on April 30, 1945. The Russian colonel who led the attack gave us a passionate account of his victory:

"The battle was terrifying. Regrouped behind sandbags, knowing they were finished, the Nazis were fighting to the death while the Russian assault force attacked bit by bit with flame throwers. The onslaught lasted several days. Separated from the main force in a basement where a bomb had exploded and penetrated the rotunda, everybody was engaged in hand to hand combat. The wounded lay scattered everywhere, and the dead, piled in the bunker, emitted a suffocating stench."

The colonel pointed out an enormous water reservoir

protected by concrete which was meant to allow for survival under prolonged siege.

He also showed us the precise location where he himself found the bodies of Goebbels, the Minister of Propaganda, and his wife and six children, all suicides. He then showed another spot where the charred bodies of Hitler and Eva Braun were found; the Führer's dentist identified the remains, confirmed thanks to Bormann's partially burned diary found at the scene in which one could make out the April 30, 1945 entry "Hitler and Eva Braun committed suicide." At the time of our visit in 1947, doubts about Hitler's suicide persisted, especially as Bormann's body was not recovered.

Having assigned Pierre to take his place presiding over international festivities for soldiers and Resistance fighters in Berlin, General Koenig welcomed us for a second time to his opulent residence situated next to a splendid lake. Each of the Allied forces participated in a show organized for the occasion. Great Britain featured Scottish dancers in a perfect performance of the Dance of the Swords. The Americans hired professional Germans to perform a quite decent variety show, while the Russians enjoyed great success with their dances and chorus. The French musicians were prevented from landing due to fog so they were replaced at the last minute by Jean Nohain and Mireille whose sweet and charming fantasy seemed insipid after the rousing liveliness and prowess of the Russian acrobats...

We returned to Umkirch in the fog on a small rather crude old military plane whose pilot, very stressed, feared constantly that he would stray from the air corridor and be strafed by Russian machine gun fire. We arrived exhausted at the chateau where the family was awaiting us.

From the start of our stay in Baden, I was concerned about the effects of this luxurious lifestyle on my children. It's easier to adjust to a rise in means than a reduction. Annette adapted right away. She took full advantage of shows and balls to which we were invited but also knew how to back me up in my duties and fulfill her responsibilities. Still, sometimes she seemed flippant in her daily behavior.

Wanting to set a good example, Pierre did not want us to use, unless really necessary, his fleet of cars. If the children needed to go to town, he required they leave at the same time he was going or to go in the steward's truck. As with the other Allied forces, the French had a tendency to abuse their privileges which shocked the Germans who wanted to turn a blind eye toward the German abuses in France. At the time of the Governor's daily morning departure, the guard was standing at attention while our intrepid Annette arrived, running full speed, dress unbuttoned and hair brush in hand!

When we had a party in town, French officials and the Germans would wait until we left to say goodnight to the Governor before leaving themselves. But it was generally Annette – never in a hurry to go home – who kept the party going and kept everyone waiting around. We finally decided not to take her home with us and to let her stay the night with friends in town, even though this was rather unusual for the time when it was still expected that a girl would be a virgin when she wed.

One persistent suitor appeared on the scene: fun, dynamic and ambitious, Paul Guillaut, nicknamed Booby, was a young lieutenant serving as ordnance officer for General Dassonville. He was attracted by our daughter's inner qualities and her petite physique – she was small statured as was he.

Annette liked his dashing spirit and his impertinence but we thought they were both very young. It seemed to us that Annette's feelings wavered, and Booby had to go to Indochina for two and a half years. When they told us of their marriage plans, we laid out the risks of such a long separation and we all agreed not to announce anything official until after his return from the Far East.

Taking Olivier for a few days to France's Midi to regain my strength following my double pneumonia, I learned of Booby's next move from Pierre: he had gone to Baden to introduce Annette to his mother and gave Annette an engagement ring. Happily this young man was lucky: of the nine graduates of St. Cyr (France's equivalent of West Point Academy) who went with him to Indochina, five were killed, three wounded, and the last perished some time later in Algeria.

When he came back, he made us change from a simple family ceremony we had planned with his mother to a large wedding at Umkirch. The occasion would be lavish.

The day of the wedding, Annette took forever getting ready. I climbed to her room where the dressmaker was adjusting her magnificent Rochas wedding dress, called the "Country Bride" ... Hesitating to put on the veil that went with the dress of "broderie anglaise" and to pin on the white orchids we had gone to great lengths to get in Alsace, she had a moment of doubt. "Do you think I am right to marry?" "That was for you to think about earlier. I beg you. Everyone is waiting for you."

After a moment of thought, Annette suddenly decided to make up for lost time, rushed down the staircase nearly losing her veil and took her place, radiant, on her father's arm at the head of the procession from the chateau to the church, admired by the onlookers.

The village women had come at dawn and festooned the door of the house, the entrance gate and the church porch with garlands and paper flowers. They had also put dust on the steps of the porch of the chateau which, according to local tradition, the bride would have to sweep.

And on the eve of the wedding, while we were having dinner with the two families and close friends in from France, the villagers came, to our great surprise, to serenade us with two orchestras, one municipal and one clerical. Keep in mind that we were the "foreign occupiers".

At the church, the village priest performed the religious service and the French chaplain gave the homily. This German-French balance was very pleasing to the many German guests representing all the institutions: university, hospital, music school, etc. I made a quick calculation of 1800 handshakes of well wishes. The gifts were abundant.

The entire village was invited back to the chateau's park where more than three buffets, a wine cask and a keg of beer were arrayed and the whole village proceeded to get drunk. "Long live the newlyweds."

Eight months later, we hosted a luncheon party with much the same guest list, in honor of a visit to Fribourg by Ambassador François-Poncet and his wife. Annette was in painful labor with her first child, Christine. Our guests from Baden, strict Catholics, discreetly counted the elapsed months on their fingers…

A beautiful young girl with regular features, Florence, sportive, balanced, self-possessed but modest, also had suitors. Five years younger than Annette, she studied psychology at the University of Strasbourg and grew close to a student from Guadalupe enrolled in the same program. Tall, brown-haired and thin, with beautiful green eyes, this former seminarian seemed to us to lack character. He wanted to marry before finishing his studies, which hardly pleased us, and counted on us to support his household which was against our principles.

Pierre and I decided to invite him to join us for a sightseeing trip to Denmark and the north of Germany. Our first impression was reinforced and I began a painful explanation to bring him around to our position. He had to have his diploma before thinking of marriage. The break-up of the two went pretty easily.

* * *

Reason trumping emotions, Florence did not rebel against us. She moved to Boulogne and then to the U.S. where she got a scholarship to Columbia University in New York. Meanwhile, she met a literary critic, Pierre de Boisdeffre, a dazzling speaker with a mediocre physique. Thirty-two years old, he thought Florence would make the perfect wife for him and decided to have us meet his parents in a superb chateau that an astute ancestor had purchased at low cost after the Revolution.

His mother was very distinguished, the daughter of général de Boisdeffre, sadly made famous at the time of the Dreyfus Affair. (As the Army Chief of Staff he was the head of those opposing to exonerate Dreyfus notwithstanding the proofs of his innocence). She tried to clear her father's name. She claimed he had been consumed by the Franco-Russian alliance and circumvented by his subordinates. The father of Pierre de Boisdeffre accepted that his son would inherit from his spinster aunt, the family name – prestigious to some, but hated by Emile Zola and other Dreyfus defenders. The marriage of his only son to a half-Jewish woman would make everyone forget that shameful episode.

During a walk, Mme. de Boisdeffre deftly asked me questions which made me realize she didn't know we had other children. In other words, she was hoping Pierre's wealth, which she assumed was concomitant with his titles, would allow us to help them update their feudal chateau with modern comforts ... Florence's imminent departure for the U.S. temporarily sidelined this problem.

Settled overseas, beautiful Florence went to Mexico at the invitation of the parents of a professor of medicine she had been seeing in New York. This new relationship, too, brought a marriage proposal. Florence decided to speak with us face to face before making any decision. On her voyage home, she ran into a young man, Elliot Rosenberg, alias Pete, Jewish and American, whom she had already met at Columbia University. The two young people would wait two years until they had finished their studies to seal their union on July 16, 1957, the anniversary of my own marriage.

Our third child, Didier, age eleven to seventeen during our stay in Baden, hated his father's official position. He was at an age when adolescents don't like to stand out from their friends. He feared compliments as well as criticisms about his parents.

His two sisters quickly learned the language of the country, taking private lessons as well as going to the theater, cinema, and enjoying the company of Germans their age; he refused to invite his friends home. And he very seriously explained to me that he felt like a prisoner at the chateau because if he wanted to go to town five miles away, he had to go in the steward's truck. In the end, that is how he learned to drive at age fourteen and never needed lessons to get his permit!

My strictness about his outings to town, checking his grades, the minimal pocket money he was allowed, in comparison to his friends who came from families of more modest means, were always sources of contention between us.

He was shocked, however, by the behavior of fellow students at the French high school who had flaunted thefts they had committed, and by the reaction of their parents; he came to me to explain that he understood the reason for our attitude. So as to avoid disgrace for the families involved, Pierre notified the parents of the thieves to submit their resignations. The latter tried in vain to justify their children's actions by explaining they were just getting back for thefts by the Nazis! No need to say more than that a review of their files during Hitler's occupation proved they were all supporters of Pétain if not worse. It was for that reason they had all been so anxious to leave France at Liberation. Pierre was aghast reading the report of the jobs these negligent parents held: policemen, teachers, low level civil servants, officers. There was even a baron!

Soon thereafter, another minor scandal erupted. A student who had overheard his parents discussing an affair between a captain and a certain Mme X tried to extort blackmail from the man. The money was to be handed over in the middle of the night on the spiral staircase to the steeple of the beautiful pink cathedral. The budding gangster found himself face to face with the French police.

As for our dear Didier, he owed me one for that Christmas at Umkirch when we annually followed the same ritual. I always prepared a big party for the village children at our house, decorated with Christmas trees in the foyer and music room; there was an average of one hundred forty gifts. My daughters helped me shop at the stores which still suffered a paucity of items on the shelves.

Faithful to his ways, then in eleventh grade, he did the least possible to get by so as to be able to be free of work for the vacation. Eight days before Christmas, he brought me his report card to sign – he had received 8 ½ and 9 ½ out of 20 in Latin assignments. Furious that he had slacked off, I decided to withhold his presents.

A few days later, Annette, Florence and I were shopping at the stores with a long list. We had second thoughts about Didier and his disappointment ... He was waiting for me when we returned home and presented me with passing grades. So happy about this turnaround, I gave him 100 marks and told him to hurry to buy the ski boots I knew he had been dreaming about before the stores closed. Vacation was near – as were the ski slopes.

The period of Christmas, feeling more like Lent in its

sparseness, marked a turning point in Didier's life. He received one after the other a prize for excellence and later honorable mention for his baccalaureate before going on to become a brilliant graduate student with multiple diplomas.

Being only three when we arrived at Umkirch, Olivier posed fewer problems. He was an easy and delectable child, doted on by his older siblings, the staff and our entire entourage. Overly gifted and modest, he surprised each successive teacher before becoming a Maoist student.

Our stay in Germany led to the chance to take a trip to Vienna and Czechoslovakia with M. Deshusse, a Swiss national who was the director of the French Institute at Fribourg, and his wife, both of whom knew central Europe well as they had lived there.

At our first stop in Vienna, we visited a famous rococo abbey overlooking the beautiful Danube which is no longer blue due to pollution. We left the abbey accompanied by an Austrian professor and came upon a Russian checkpoint. We stopped. A soldier with a machine gun threatened us despite the French flag on the car. Getting into the vehicle, which already held seven people, he had the gate opened to the Russian HQ and it closed again behind us. A Romanian vehicle was similarly detained in this small courtyard where soldiers were playing a strange game with logs.

During our walk in town, the Austrian professor, a friend of the Deshusses, told us of the savagery of the Russian occupation forces, indicating that thousands of Austrian women had to be treated in the hospital for rapes by Soviet soldiers. Mme Bargeton, the wife of Pierre's chief of staff, and Mme Deshusse were shaking with fear but Annette and I remained calm. The wait continued while our three companions were taken inside the villa. After many long minutes, they finally came out and we were taken without further explanation out of the forbidden zone, still under the scrutiny of the armed guard.

The reason for our detention became clear. Having left our passports at the consulate to get the entry visas for Czechoslovakia, we had no papers which made us suspicious in the eyes of the Russians; they had to copy their report on us seven times because of the lack of a typewriter!

The next day we arrived in Prague and toured this admirable city, liberated from the Nazi yoke only to fall into Russian hands six months later ...

A dinner with Czech academics, friends of the Deshusses, enlightened us on the local mood: "Ours is a pivotal country in need of friends in the West as well as the East to maintain balance. The Russians, Slavs like us, were, after all, our liberators."

A year after that evening, we learned that practically all had been arrested in February during a Communist putsch which our Ambassador to Prague, M Dejean, explained was hardly a cause for rejoicing. He could no longer greet Czech acquaintances he had known before the seizure for risk of them being taken away. The Russians crushed Bohemia and Moravia like a swarm of locusts. Stores were totally emptied out and factories were dismantled and sent to Russia.

Another journey gave us the chance to visit Berchtesgaden, Hitler's infamous eagle's nest in the American zone. We had let them know we were coming and the Americans organized a low key welcome. We were put up in a comfortable room and enjoyed delicious meals and an evening of dancing during which I couldn't help but notice that our friends from the other side of the Atlantic only danced in very tight embrace.

We of course visited the peak where Chamberlain and Daladier were received in September 1938 for the signing of the infamous Munich Agreement. We recalled how we had wept when we learned of this decision, understanding the trap that would spring on us. Daladier himself, contrite at having bowed to Nazi pressure, was stunned when he was welcomed back to France by a crowd that did not understand.

After our visit to the place that had witnessed this sinister agreement, we headed to a strangely beautiful and mysterious lake. A gorgeous yacht was tied up at the shore and we asked Pierre's chief of staff to inquire if it could be rented for a tour.

"This boat is reserved for a high level person".

"Who? I said. "Ask him."

"A French Governor, Pierre Pène."

Delighted by this excursion of which we had not been aware, we nonetheless concluded that the discretion of our American hosts was maybe a bit excessive. Still, we warmly thanked them before leaving.

We had regular contact with the American Governor and his entourage based in Stuttgart, and we attended the national holiday festivities of each other. But in our six years in Baden, we hardly had the chance to establish personal relationships because the American Governors changed frequently.

Prior to relations with the Germans being authorized by high level French authorities, our landlords, the Prince and Princess of Hohenzollern, tried to establish inroads with us. Our very sociable daughters invited a number of friends home, many, of course, French but also friends passing through and stateless people from the Baltic countries which had been invaded first by the Nazis, then by the Russians. They quickly won the affection of a son and nephew of the Prince. Understandably, the young men wanted to enjoy the fabulous parties, swimming in the pool, canoe rides on the pond and tennis games, with our daughters who were the same age.

One year, the Prince and Princess of Hohenzollern invited us for a New Year's Eve party. Put in an awkward spot by the invitation, we decided to have our daughters attend in our place.

All German nobility were there, taking their time at the buffet. The conviviality soon gave way to drunkenness and our daughters, both very sober and feeling a bit as if on an official mission, hesitated to leave. Unsure of what might happen, the Princess told them both to slip away to escape this orgy. Annette and Florence hurried back across the park to tell us about their evening and German excess when it came to parties. Pierre and I had had a similar experience with a group of Germans in Ethiopia.

Some time later, in September of 1950, our landlords' eldest son was married, about the same time Annette married Booby. The Princess brought us a lovely photo of the sumptuous wedding which took place in the Thurn and Taxis castle. A footman in Louis XV regalia attended each guest. The chandeliers and sparkling silver candelabras provided a magical illumination of the gathering of all German and Austrian royalty. But in the end, two months later, a distraught Princess Margaret came to tell me the drama of this brilliant marriage which her son had failed to consummate. She felt the humiliation more than the Thurn and Taxis family (whose fortune had been made from a large postal service a century earlier), which remained the wealthiest noble family in Germany.

Not long before their break-up, the father of the unfortunate bride had invited himself to a party for young people, organized by our daughters, and told me "I know this is not an evening for adults but I feel very young!" He invited us to visit him soon at his extraordinary castle but, unfortunately, we never found the time or opportunity to do so…

When André François-Poncet became France's first Ambassador to the German Federal Republic, he set himself up in Bonn in an expensive house that had been a luxurious meeting place before Germany's defeat. The property was well suited to entertaining guests but lacked the charm of Umkirch where Napoleon himself had stayed.

Mme François-Poncet was the most likeable and competent hostess one could meet and received us well, helping us make a tour of the chateaux of the region. As for her husband, we already knew of his brilliant conversation and caustic personality; we had had the opportunity to host him at Umkirch.

Following our first three day visit during which Pierre met Adenauer and a number of other German ministers, we were invited to the Ambassador's home for many years to follow for New Year's festivities, catching a special train every December 31st from Baden to Bonn.

General Guillaume's ordnance officer, responsible for putting up guests in conformance with strict protocol, always put us in a good spot. As with the other Governors, for example Boislambert representing the north and Widmer the east, we were entitled to a drawing room and sleeping car.

One year as we were setting down our bags, we found in our spot Monsignor Picard de la Vacquerie, the bishop of the French zone. Taking great care in fulfilling his mission, the young officer accompanying us politely ejected the bishop.

"I have to change my robe" he objected.

"So do I" I replied.

We would later learn that young seminarians, sensitive about the bishop's reputation – which very quickly became known throughout our entourage – sent out a humorous note to those likely to entertain the bishop, libeling him as follows: "As Monsignor follows a strict regimen, please be so kind as to serve him only caviar, lobster, foie gras and the like."

We were not aware of this note prior to a visit from this curious fellow as he made his way to Freibourg for Confirmations... and was received by Pierre and Florence for a

catastrophic luncheon. First, he arrived quite late – a car following
him had hit a German bicyclist. He was in a terrible mood, having
been seated to Florence's right instead of face to face with the
Governor. He sought in vain for my fifteen year old daughter to
reassure him about his mediocre sermon. And he ate poorly since
our cook had collapsed at the stove after drinking the good
burgundy I had provided for the coq au vin.

I couldn't be there as I was convalescing at Sainte-Maxime,
having almost died November 11, 1947 of double pneumonia.
The saving penicillin had just arrived with the American
occupation in Germany. The professor summoned by the doctor
was testing it for the first time and said in front of me that he
wasn't sure he could save me.

Before leaving Germany in 1952 we would entertain seven
hundred more people in the course of two garden parties. German
emotions were frayed, fearful of being left alone to face the
Russians. They were also sorry to see us go because they liked us.

Pierre missed this incredible assignment, a great honor and a
passion, where he could demonstrate all his capabilities. As for
me, worn out from the social demands, I was not sorry to leave
this beautiful chateau and return to our little apartment in
Boulogne.

Upon returning to Paris, Pierre took several steps to find a
position commensurate with his exceptional potential. He realized
how much his peers had envied his postings as Commissaire of
the Republic and Governor of Baden which had been handed to
him on a platter thanks to his role in the Resistance.

It was a given that he found a job to put food on the table at
the Ministry for Reconstruction but the government rewarded his
colleagues from the French Zone even though they had had less
of an impact than Pierre. That was how Boislambert was named
Chancellor of the Liberation by de Gaulle, and Widmer first got a

position at the House of Representatives, and later at the Ministry of War.

Still, Pierre's accomplishments were such that, some twenty years after our departure, Chancellor Brandt decorated him with the highest level of the German Order of Merit, at the request of the son of a former Minister of Baden. The German Ambassador in Paris organized a brilliant reception in Pierre's honor, in a beautiful hotel decorated by Eugène de Beauharnais. We were permitted to make our own guest list.

This award, paired with that of the "Compagnon de la Libération", proved, if need be, Pierre's worth, courage and charisma. He was at the same time simple and self-confident and very manly. Women chased after him – when he was young because of his dance skills, later because of his capabilities. He himself told me this later, when I had become his priority.

Although secondary, my role as spouse of the Governor also carried a certain importance.

I knew how to put guests at ease, encourage (on orders of the Minister of Foreign Affairs) contacts with the Germans, including their spouses at gatherings where they could meet politicians, artists, and academics.

A genius from Freibourg, who won the Nobel Prize in chemistry, told us during a visit to Paris that he had attended a huge celebration of the 400th anniversary of the University of Fribourg and that, not since our departure, had he had such an opportunity to interact with his colleagues! He also seemed surprised by our modest Boulogne apartment after the luxury of Umkirch. It was a way to demonstrate that the occupation officials, at least some, had not taken advantage of their position to get rich.

I was pleasantly surprised in 1992 – still living while Pierre had been dead for twenty years – by the loyalty of staff personnel at all levels who still thought about me after all those years.

Pierre Pène and his four children

NINE

IN SERVICE OF
THE PRINCE OF MONACO

Following the luxury of our time in Baden, the family resumed its middle class and rather thrifty lifestyle. Only Annette still lived in Germany, adapting to her new role as the wife of a young officer.

She would later regain her independence thanks to yoga which she made her life's work. She was an athlete who always needed to exert herself with a work out.

Following her attendance at New York's Columbia University, Florence became a psychologist and took a job teaching female juvenile delinquents, a difficult career which did not even leave her with weekends free and which paid barely a maid's wages. Her director, a small, nervous, passionate woman, made drama over all the problems that arose in this home for young women, most frequently as a result of pimps trying to lure them to work as streetwalkers.

Florence did very well – perhaps too well. The director, a bit unsure of herself, took advantage, unburdening herself and crying on Florence's shoulder. Seeing Florence, so young and beautiful, the young women were drawn to her. Without really understanding why, they leaned on my daughter to learn to swim in the pool, to sew, or even to learn English.

Florence made the effort to contact potential employers for jobs for them as secretaries and also contacting the judges managing the girls' cases.

Conscious of the service she was rendering but also of how little the job was doing for her, she soon wanted a change and was eventually hired by Philips where she worked until the arrival of her fiancé, Pete Rosenberg.

Pierre was wilting away at the Ministry of Reconstruction where he had no responsibility. He was thrown a bone to chew on for a month and a half. It was a mission to the UN; he wanted the chance to show me the U.S., a powerful and dynamic country.

On a break from Janson-de-Sailly High School, Didier was cramming for exams for entry at the highly competitive "Ecole Normale Supérieure". He really seemed to want to pursue studies in political science and get into the "Ecole Nationale d'Administration".

Enrolled since our return from Germany at Claude Bernard high school, Olivier got off on the wrong foot with an elderly math professor because of his poor penmanship – his writing was chicken scratch. Three months later, I was summoned by his English teacher, who seemed embarrassed:

"First, your son surprised me by being at the head of the English class even though many of my students have a British mother or governess. But when we reviewed his dossier at the roundtable of all the professors, whatever the subject was, Olivier knew it. Although never flaunting himself in class, he would raise his hand if nobody else did, invariably answering the question with the correct answer. In fact, he was the only student in four sections of classes to discover an error purposely presented by the math professor. What is your husband's profession? When he filled out a form at the beginning of the year, Olivier wrote 'works on the reconstruction'. Might he be Polytechnicien?"

Ah, the satisfied smile of a proud mother ...

"Yes, in fact. In addition we have lived abroad and his brother and sisters each pursued different paths, which have led to Olivier's diverse interests."

Back at home I told Pierre about the meeting. Olivier had shown him the math problem in question. "It's an error in logic, not calculation, that he uncovered, which is remarkable for someone his age!" Pushing me to tell Olivier that the error had been purposefully presented by the professor, I heard my future revolutionary respond: "Then why did he give me a grade of only 4 out of 20?" Good question, I said to myself.

Always animated, the discussions at our dinner table were often contentious, especially with Didier, trained by his studies to dissect all layers of issues in general and, in particular, our political opinions. "Get in the game, mom", he said one day when I asked for mercy. "I am at an age where it's important to develop my own personality and stop reflecting yours."

He was right. His sisters, older and closer, had overshadowed his childhood until Annette's marriage. He got along better with Florence who was calmer, less authoritative and who, on the eve of his baccalaureate exam, encouraged him to review certain subjects from four years prior. This wise advice allowed him to succeed brilliantly on the test, earning an honorable mention.

His father imposed on Didier his self worth, his past career, and his role as head of the family, the weight of which I felt as well.

Thanks to friends of the President of Baden, M. Wohleb, who became Germany's Ambassador to Portugal, it was suggested we spend the summer vacation of 1954 in a comfortable apartment in Lisbon for a reasonable price.

This lovely plan was cancelled just as we were about to leave because Pierre was named to the cabinet of M. Chaban-Delmas, then Minister of Public Works during the brief Presidency of Mendès-France who sought to straighten out finances and the Chamber of Deputies. Pierre couldn't refuse and sacrificed the vacation to modestly contribute to this undertaking.

Honest, brilliant, stubborn, self-assured, Mendès-France, opposed by many adversaries, unfortunately had to leave office after only seven months and Pierre fell, once again, between the cracks. He felt too old and too loyal to stay on in the intrigue-ridden cabinet of Chaban's successor, the aviator Corniglion-Molinier.

He went back to his dusty office at the Porte Dauphine which he shared with a decent civil servant.

In 1955, with the help of an employee who had worked for Pierre in Germany, we rented a villa near Cassis. I learned to make soup with fish caught each morning by one of the two sons of the villa's owner and had free use of the fruits and vegetables from the garden. That summer, spent at the seaside just next to forested countryside, was marvelous.

Upon returning to Paris, Pierre headed straight to the Ministry where no one told him anything in particular, while I unpacked and thanked a neighbor who had watered the plants in our absence. She advised me of our next departure, to Monte Carlo, showing me the newspaper: "My son read in Le Monde that, following the scandals at Monte Carlo's Precious Metals Bank, the

French government appointed Pierre Penne (sic) as advisor of Public Works, that is to say Minister in the Principality."

When we were in Cassis, Pierre and I had read a brief reference to the situation in the local paper. I had even mentioned that it would be a good post for him. "I feel too action-oriented for a patronage job like this. My colleagues would make fun of me."

Furious to have learned of his nomination in such an unofficial way, Pierre hurried to see the personnel director who was surprised by his reaction.

"But after all, you were at the Cote d'Azur this summer?"

"I don't see what that has to do with it."

"Surely you took steps to seek your selection for the post?"

"Absolutely not. I know nothing about Monaco's government and anyway have no intention of accepting this post."

"You can't do that! The decision was made by the Council of Ministers. You were placed at the top of a list of three names suggested to the Prince who chose you because of your résumé. To turn it down would be an insult. And understand that you will pay no taxes, and you will receive housing with servants and a chauffeured car. A lot of your colleagues would love to be in your place."

Only the tax advantage would materialize and only during the term of the assignment. The other benefits were reserved for the lone Minister of State who always had to be French, and who was generally chosen from the diplomatic or prefectorial corps. According to the agreements between France and the Principality, these advantages did not extend to the Ministries of Interior, Finance and Public Works, of which two had to be Monacan and one French. This latter requirement had been overlooked until the infamous scandal. Those in said positions, having fought in the war against Germany, had thus earned dual French and Monacan nationality.

After a fortnight of hesitation, during which Pierre was sullen and irritable, he finally accepted the nomination. We left for Monaco a month later with Olivier, age thirteen, and our granddaughter, Patricia, who was only eighteen months old. Her parents, Annette and Booby, had left for Algeria which was erupting, and preferred to leave their daughters with their grandmothers, bringing with them only their poor mentally handicapped son, Gilles.

When we arrived, the Minister of State, M. Soum, lazy and proud of it, immodestly vaunted the privileges of his position. That didn't prevent him from pleasing the sovereign who obviously appreciated Soum's gift of impersonation and his recurring cynicism. During a diplomatic luncheon, he went so far as to tell us that he had pursued his career without ever working, so as to never be criticized. When he retired, the Prince created a job for him as Minister in Switzerland in a town in which not a single Monacan resided ... which did not fail to make the common people complain.

His successor, M. Pelletier, whom we already knew, seemed more serious and we congratulated ourselves on his arrival. This former minister of General de Gaulle was not as interesting as one might think. He seemed jealous of Pierre's effectiveness, probably remembering with bitterness that he was only "Préfet" for the Seine area when Pierre was "Commissaire de la République" for the area where he himself had held the post of regional prefect under the Vichy government. He did not ask the Prince to extend Pierre's contract through to retirement. That would have meant an extension of two years and would have allowed Pierre to finish projects begun under his tenure. An example was the move of two enormous gas tanks on unstable ground at Cap d'Ail and another, the difficult construction of a magnificent pool at the port "la Condamine", a location where mine removal was required.

Pierre had also been part of the reconstruction plan for the Principality, imposing strict limits on the height of buildings. While the early undertakings were completed as established projects, the long range urbanization plans, notably the terraced floor structures my husband had argued in favor of, were not respected.

In an attempt at self-preservation, M. Pelletier, unlike Pierre, turned a blind eye to dubious schemes, one of which caused a huge uproar. In 1955 when the bank scandal that spawned Pierre's appointment erupted, the French government and a businessman bought the shares of the Bank of Precious Metals in order to ward off the Principality's bankruptcy.

The sale of gold not being permitted at the time, the bank had played the arbitrage of the price of gold on the Swiss, Italian and Monacan markets. When the purchase was made legal and markets dropped, Pastor, a major entrepreneur of Italian origin and a recently naturalized Monacan citizen, anticipated the coming sale. He withdrew an enormous sum from the bank, setting off panic and a bank run. To prevent this disaster, the Prince decided to take, in violation of the French-Monacan agreements, financial measures which he delegated to M. Pelletier. Learning of this scheme, the civil servant for Monacan affairs at the Quai d'Orsay picked up the phone and ordered M. Pelletier to immediately have the decision rescinded.

It was 11 p.m. when Pelletier went to see Rainier III who was surrounded by his usual guests. He was coldly shown the door.

It was the beginning of a long dispute between the two countries. The perks of the French who had resided in Monaco for more than five years were cancelled. The Prince upheld the tax exemption for his subjects and foreigners – except the French – by order of de Gaulle. Little by little, the two countries found a way to work with each other again, but the hapless Pelletier had earned the Prince's rancor as well as that of his subjects, and the anger of the French. His predecessor, M. Soum, had only been hated by the Monacans.

"Here you will always be considered a foreigner" M. Pelletier told Pierre one day.

Despite the ties and the language that united us, the Monacans were more proud than if they were truly French.

Their sovereign, a Grimaldi bearing a name nine centuries old, brought them a lustrous image, particularly in the US. The Genovese ancestors of Prince Rainier were pirates. Perhaps that's where the sovereign got his taste for material wealth for himself and his minuscule 375 acre nation.

A great admirer of American achievement, the Prince launched his state into exaggerated modernity. For him it was a fundamental requirement. He succeeded at the expense of aesthetics and charm. Luxury replaced seduction. Proportionally speaking, his powers exceeded those of the Queen of England, who had to submit herself to the directives of the Prime Minister.

After the death of his grandfather, Rainier III, a bit intoxicated with his power, played with people, elevating or demoting them according to his whims, at the same time appropriating the salaries of those who were discarded. He had no hesitation in dismissing two consecutive Assemblies which had dared to criticize him a bit too overtly. In a year-end address, he argued that his fall from power would relegate the Principality to the status of a French sub-prefecture. His former subjects would have to pay taxes and their sons would be obliged to do military service. His warnings were well taken.

He was thirty-three years old and had been on the throne for five years when we arrived. Still, he was a bit unsure of himself, for example re-knotting his tie before receiving visitors. Self-conscious of his inferior education, he kept a distance from those he admired most, such as the Bishop of Monaco and my husband, receiving them frequently but officially, using strict protocol to avoid personal conversations.

He was more at ease with his childhood friends who profited a bit too much from his loyal friendship. They did not have very good reputations and proved to be bad advisors. He also preferred the company of the infamous Soum, a very touchy fellow but a great impersonator, ridiculing all around him, entertaining the Prince.

His personal confessor, Fr. Tucker, was also his advisor. He loved the Prince and Princess and had a real fondness for money. At St. Charles of Monte Carlo Cathedral, he never failed to mention their names and the collection. An odd person, he was forced to disappear when rumors surfaced about his inappropriate relationships with his young students. Despite Fr. Tucker's insistence, Olivier, who was one of them, refused to see him without us.

But Tucker was not without good points. It was he who arranged Rainier's marriage, instigating his break-up with his girl-friend at the time, the charming actress Gisèle Pascal. He confided to us one day that he had met her at St.-Jean-Cap-Ferrat and concluded: "She is charming but couldn't interest Rainier, a sovereign, or even me, a priest! Grace Kelly, by contrast, has the good luck to combine her celebrity, beauty, kindness and wealth. Besides, she knows how to bring stable happiness to the Prince and to make him aware of his rights and, especially, his responsibilities."

As soon as he arrived on the scene, Pierre, aided by two assistants who explained the arcane ways of the country, got down to business. As in any government, intrigue teemed around the Prince. Pierre had seen it in Ethiopia and in Chaban-Delmas' cabinet. Still, he was surprised by the magnitude of the local gossip and schemes where everything was obfuscated. If they were talking about the Prince, people used code words. In the National

Assembly, his name was not to be uttered.

Being responsible for Public Works and therefore the largest part of the budget, Pierre was constantly called on the carpet. Each of his deputies knew he was not responsible for any abuses but such are the rules of the game. Teaming up with his staff director and chief engineer, both honest and hard-working, he tried to anticipate problems so as to avoid them ...

With the help of Pierre's staff director, Raymond Biancheri, I was able to find a recently renovated furnished rental apartment on the port when we arrived. Given its price and poor quality, we decided to buy a 1000 sq foot place with an unobstructed view. My search took six months to find what we wanted.

Although we really were taken by the areas of Cap-Ferrat, Saint-Martin and Roquebrune, we resigned ourselves to buy within the Principality so as to benefit from the tax free privilege that would come after five years of residence ... It was impossible to anticipate the break between de Gaulle and the Principality.

After seventy-five visits here and there, I finally found, thanks to the president of the National Council, an old apartment, un-renovated but on the water. It cost us six million francs of the day to which would be added three million in renovation costs.

As usual, Pierre gave me carte blanche, sending me a pleasant and honest architect who got me good craftsmen. The work started and we decided to take Olivier to the countryside, to Saint-Martin-de-Vésubie near Nice, anticipating we would move in in late September.

When we got there, Olivier decided to climb a peak near the hotel. I persuaded him to wait for Didier who was coming to stay with us following a stay in Austria. An inexplicable and foreshadowing anxiety came over me, churning my stomach, as I watched the two boys head for the mountain. It was a grey day and drizzling lightly. All of a sudden, I frightfully remembered the fatal fall of one of my friends who had gone on an excursion, against her own wishes, to please her father.

Waiting for their return more or less the whole day, I finally saw Olivier at about 5 p.m. He was running toward me, his face contorted.

"Come quickly" he cried, "Didier has broken his leg." We went right away with a stretcher, accompanied by the hotel owner. When, at seven years old, Olivier had had a similar accident, I had not had the worrying premonition. It happened while skiing and I took him to the emergency room in Fribourg where a ninety year old German surgeon took charge.

Seven years later, I was in an ambulance at my other son's side. He was suffering. In Nice, two surgeons arrived and examined the young man. They were two tipsy colleagues who had just returned from dinner. One was Dr. Decamps from Nice, the other Dr. Orrechia of Monaco who had a dubious reputation which would follow him until 1980. To myself, I referred to them as Mutt and Jeff ...

During the surgery to set Didier's femur and close the wound, I paced anxiously. According to these doctors, Didier would be able to resume in three months his studies at "Science Politique" where he had just been admitted, having been accepted as well at the "Ecole Normale Supérieure" at the Rue d'Ulm. I didn't believe it.

The clinic left a lot to be desired. Didier fussed constantly, worrying about his studies. The radiologist, son of the clinic's owner, kept messing up the X-rays ... and I made the mistake of paying the bills presented to me too promptly. His fees paid, the surgeon quickly lost interest in Didier and released him to me to return to Monaco.

At the same time, I had a lump in my breast and went immediately to Paris to be operated on by the famous Dr. Taillefer, who had already removed one malignant tumor for me two years earlier. I was only hospitalized for three days and returned to Monaco, drain in my breast, to take care of Didier and oversee the work on our future apartment.

After a few weeks, Didier left to resume his studies with the approval of Dr. Decamps. We soon realized that a staph infection had set in under his closed incision. The clinic was poorly maintained and we had been poorly informed.

It was the beginning of a long and painful episode for our son, with relapses and treatments over three long and anxiety-ridden years. In the end, Dr. Trillat of Lyon, as serious and brilliant as Dr. Taillefer, would save his leg by taking the risk of doing a bone graft on his infected bone. Our son, in the clinic, did not take well to this interruption of his studies. We went as often as possible to see him in Briançon, where the clean air was good for him. All alone he worked, sometimes with his father. He had to change his plans because of age limits in his desired program but got a scholarship from Stanford University which allowed him to earn a respected and practical diploma.

During these years of constant upheaval, Pierre was doing battle in the snake pit of Monaco. Instead of being the cushy job he had feared at the outset, this posting was turning out to be the most difficult of his career. To it, he added a personal problem that turned stupidly legal.

Returning from the religious service that concluded the marriage of Prince Rainier III to Grace Kelly, following a series of receptions to which we had been invited along with all European and American society, we were finally resting at home when the thunder of a waterfall made us jump.

A pipe in the bathroom had burst. Water was rapidly rising and it was impossible to turn off the main without the concierge who wasn't there. It was a holiday in honor of the Prince's marriage! So we called the fire department which took some time to stop the deluge. Although the managing agent, the insurance company and the architect all attributed the break to faulty construction, the owner of the apartment took us to court. After losing the proceeding, she appealed, lost again, and refused to pay our legal expenses. After two and a half years of useless bother, our court win cost us almost as much as if we had directly paid for the repairs to the bookstore below us! ... In the meantime, we managed to move into our new apartment, completely renovated to my careful specifications. And I got down to the business of taking care of Patricia who had arrived completely anemic with her poor bowed legs and distended stomach.

The regimen was simple: gradual exposure to sunshine on the balcony in winter, heated salt water baths on the terrace, fortifying food, and swimming lessons. At twenty-two months of age, Patricia swam and dove in the large pool, setting an example for older children in the class. We took her to the Beach, the Principality's elegant spot where famous people from around the world came to relax. We appreciated this oasis where high prices prevented overcrowding in July and August. At first, the snob appeal amused us. It would quickly lose its allure and I soon stopped going.

Because of Pierre's job, we got free admission and paid half price for a private cabana. Not only would this privilege cease at the end of his contract but the director, who had always kowtowed to us, gave our cabana away without even asking if we wanted to pay full price to keep it! Our downstairs neighbor, Chiron, a former race car driver, who had invited us to his annual cocktail party and bowed to us, also changed his attitude at the end of Pierre's contract, even going as far as to make an anti-Semitic remark: "Go back to your kibbutz" he told me one day.

This pretentious and famous man had started out as a valet at the hôtel de Paris, then, according to rumors, pursued his rise as a gigolo in order to buy a car.

An adorable child, Pat brought us pure joy while Olivier, a tall and thin adolescent and a brilliant student, teased me that I shouldn't spoil her too much. When at three years of age Patricia returned to her parents in Algeria, she had become a superb child.

Less occupied than in Germany with official obligations, we still had many. The Principality was a hub of meetings, shows, elegant parties and fundraising galas. Besides occasional receptions such as the Prince's marriage, there were scheduled parties such as the annual one in November for his birthday. The Rose Festival at the Opera took place in January with a very fine dinner dance and was followed by another dinner dance a few weeks later for the racers and officials of the Grand Prix of Monaco. The most ostentatious of all, attracting the millionaires of the Côte d'Azur, took place at the Summer Casino, presided over by the Highnesses, for the benefit of the Monacan Red Cross.

Added to all these society affairs were two ballet seasons at Christmas and Easter as well as opera and theater in January and February.

After being enchanted with such pomp and elegance at the beginning of our stay, it began to wear thin bit by bit ... it would have transformed without a doubt into drudgery if we had stayed longer than the five years of the official posting.

The greatest satisfaction of our stay would be, in reality, the beauty of the countryside, the view of the sea from the corniches, or even from our windows, from which we could watch the regattas and savor each day the delicately changing colors of the water. For the children, it was also the beach games, fireworks, costume parties on the "Rocher" and public dances.

Still, more than elsewhere, despite the modern aspect of new construction, I would always have the feeling that the Principality symbolized a world that was defunct, compensated, it is true, by their serene Highnesses' conviviality.

When Pierre, now a simple tourist, was hospitalized following a heart attack, he received a superb fruit basket from the Princess which would earn him pampering at the clinic.

Eight years later, when he died, the children and I received a really nice letter of condolence from Prince Rainier.

TEN

TAKING UP PAINTING AGAIN

At the end of his contract, after being there for five years, Pierre lost his benefits. Typically, an outgoing official would have been named to an honorary post with benefits extended for life but Pierre, unlike several of his predecessors had refused to become embroiled in the intrigues of Monte Carlo.

His principal obligation was to prevent bribery, which did not please everyone. When he returned to France, the Ministry of Foreign Affairs applauded him. During his five year tenure in Monaco, there had not been a single scandal.

So we resumed our life in Paris, punctuated by visits to Monaco where we had retained our apartment and continued to pursue some of our pastimes such as swimming in the sea.

On the other hand, I had to go in search of new housing in Paris – the Guillauts were living in our apartment in the rue de la Tourelle in Boulogne. So for six months we stayed in new middle income housing in Chatillon-sous-Bagneux ... a sad and banal place we were eager to leave.

Using all my energy to find a rare gem, I found a building under construction, well situated, in Boulogne. We bought a small apartment with a nice terrace and a separate room for Didier who wanted to be close to us while maintaining his independence. It was the fourteenth home since our marriage ... and I took as much pleasure as ever in employing my decorating talents, regretting at the same time that space allowed me to keep only an old armoire and chest that had belonged to my mother.

Pierre, by seniority and choice, was appointed Inspector General of Roads and Bridges. He made inspection trips to the provinces for the Minister of Public Works. As for me, after so many years of supporting my husband in his professional life and raising my four children, I took up painting again, which I had not pursued much during our marriage.

In July of 1962, knowing already that he had been accepted at "Polytechnique", Olivier had also applied to the prestigious "Ecole Normale Supérieure". The wait for the results weighed heavily on him. One Sunday afternoon, talking with us about his oral exam in chemistry, he mentioned the name of his examiner, Serge David, who had asked if he knew Pierre and Françoise Pène.

The past came rushing back to us ... Serge was the younger brother of a school friend of mine. We ran into him again in Boulogne during the Occupation, completely absorbed in preparing for his "agrégation" competition to become a professor.

But he was also the godfather, apparently forgotten, of Olivier who was born in 1943 at the height of the war. We certainly did not want to compromise any of our Resistance friends by asking them to the little baptismal ceremony my mother-in-law had insisted take place, so we had chosen Serge for his neutrality. The tumultuous period that followed bore out that reasoning; Pierre was arrested and escaped and I was imprisoned at Fresnes. As for Serge, he fled to stay with his brother-in-law in the Alps upon learning that the Vichy government was summoning students to go as "volunteer workers" to Germany. Thus contact between us was lost.

That same Sunday, the eve of the publication of exam results, Serge David telephoned the house. The reunion was warm. He told us Olivier had come in fourth out of thirty applicants admitted.

In August of 1965, the day after our return to Monaco following a long winter in Paris, Pierre suffered a massive and painful heart attack which put him in the hospital for many weeks, in danger of dying. Two months of hospitalization was followed by a long recovery, entailing a strict diet and lots of attentive care which got rid of the cause of his suffering and ten surplus pounds. But Pierre's body was tired and I begged him to give up his business travel and stressful meetings. He pushed back, assuring me he could lighten his workload without giving it up completely. For the first time, apart from the terrible period of our arrests, I realized that Pierre, my rock, might precede me in death. Death suddenly seemed very near for my life-long partner. The thought of living without him terrified me. He had not thought about death during this dangerous time. "I was sure I would beat it" he confided to me some months later.

We closely followed politics, contemporary literature and exhibitions. During this time, Annette went back to Germany with Paul, and Florence was living in Boston.

Our Olivier, age twenty-two, was as melancholic as always. He succeeded in everything he did ... but still carried the weight of the world on his shoulders and could not content himself with his accomplishments. What could I do to instill in him a love of life? I could only admire him while at the same time pitying him for his moral exigencies which would lead him to Maoism and distance him from us.

Didier took the misery of the world less seriously. He took advantage of what life had to offer, living in the moment, so happy for his freedom after three grueling years in the clinic following his accident on the mountain. Olivier remained altruistic, generous and affectionate, yet still I thought he was distancing himself from me while his older brother, as he aged, grew closer, more tender and protective.

Because Pierre was a "Compagnon de la Libération", we were invited every other year on June 18th to the Elysée Palace gardens. One year, General de Gaulle, recently operated on for cataracts, was calling out the names of his guests. A friend had forewarned Pierre that the General, discouraged by his physical state and the attacks against him, was considering leaving office as he had done in January 1946. Knowing the esteem in which the General held Pierre, the friend asked him to intervene with the General to boost his morale.

As we were preparing to leave, we found a moment alone with him. Aware that he wasn't able to see well, Pierre said: "I am Pierre Pène. Don't leave, General, the country still needs you."

Taking him affectionately by the shoulder, the General replied: "Thank you, Pène, you are very kind."

He ducked into an interior staircase trying to hide the tears that were streaming down his cheeks.

The following day, at the ceremony on June 18th in memory of the Résistance, the President, loudly cheered, had lost the bitter and disillusioned countenance of the previous day.

Earlier, just after the war, when Pierre had a chance to be near the General during meals for the "Commissaires" of the Republic or other occasions, he found him very approachable and even accepting of disagreement. It was often his majestic bearing, self-assuredness and tall stature that silenced his audience, not to mention the power of his words.

Passionate about military tactics and very familiar with the area where the General's tanks had pierced the German lines, near Montcornet and Abbeville in May 1940, Pierre could talk to him at length and attest to the care he had taken to save his soldiers' lives.

We remained very attached to the General even though we deplored some of the positions he took in 1966 and 1967, notably as regards Israel. We feared he was aging badly, as had the sadly infamous Marechal Pétain. His death in 1970 only burnished his reputation for great intellect, which he had enjoyed to the end. His successors and other party leaders would continue constantly to reference Gaullism ... forgetting sometimes that the great man, it is true, sometimes equivocated according to events, but always had the courage of his convictions.

Already having several good paintings to show, I got busy preparing an exhibition that would take place at the Gallery of Fine Arts on March 10, 1966, Pierre's sixty-eighth birthday. For the first time, I had to prepare a lithograph which would be used for the exhibit's posters. It was a delicate undertaking, requiring the use of a limited palette and thus preventing subtle shading. After ten days of trying, my entourage had varying critiques. I also had to order a box of invitations after finding someone to prepare a text describing the exhibition. My friend, the sculptress Anna Quinquaud, suggested her neighbor, an academician and art critic, Charles Kunstler.

GALERIE MARCEL BERNHEIM
35, Rue La Boëtie, PARIS 8° — Tél. ELY 11-46

FRANÇOISE PÈNE

EXPOSITION
du ██ Juin au ██ Juin inclus
16   27
VERNISSAGE LE ~~VENDREDI 13 JUIN à 16 h.~~
MARDI 16 JUIN à 16 h.

de 10 h. à 12 h.   Dimanches et
et de 14 à 18 h. 30   Lundis acceptés

FRANÇOISE PÈNE
PEINTURES ET GOUACHES

[handwritten text]

Daniel-Rops.

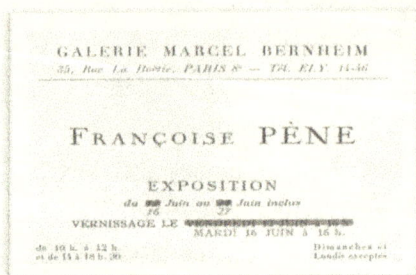

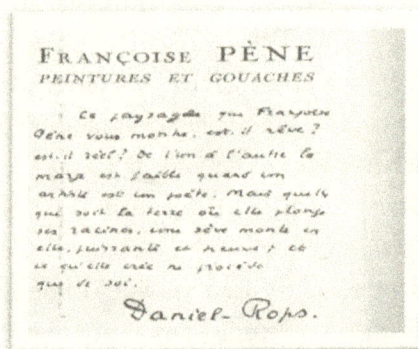

> *This landscape Françoise displays makes us ask, "Is it a dream? Is it reality?" The boundary between the two is thin when an artist is a poet. But whatever the ground in which she thrusts her roots, vigor rises up in her, powerful and fresh, and what she creates comes only from within herself.*

This hand-written critique of Françoise's paintings was written by Daniel-Rops, pen name of Henri Petiot, a renowned writer and historian of religion.

Olivier wanted me to reproduce my portrait of his father for the lithograph. The director of the gallery, the painter Vytautas Kasiulis, counseled against that, because lithographs of subjects of too personal a nature do not sell well. Having been toyed with by gallery directors when he first arrived in France, this Lithuanian refugee decided to start selling paintings himself. Thanks to his beautiful talent, folkloric and poetic, he firmly established himself, especially in Sweden and the U.S.. He unfortunately lost his spontaneity to the fumes of alcohol ... to forget the agony of his mother who had been persecuted by the Communists, as well as his own forced exile.

Another friend, Antanas Moncys, a Lithuanian sculptor, refused any compromise in his art. After making his first wife live in misery, he survived with the help of a German woman, a professor at the Goethe Institute, who became his second wife and bore him two more children.

The weeks passed and I failed to fix my lithographs, unable for technical reasons to imbue them with the poetry that one finds in my paintings.

The fine arts academician, Kunstler, whom I wanted to ask to write the text for my show, got himself wrapped up in a strange adventure. This seventy-five year old bachelor allowed himself to be sucked in by a twenty-eight year old young woman who married him for entree into the art world. He was embroiled in a domestic drama.

So I decided to contact Florence's former suitor, Pierre de Boisdeffre, the literary critic and author of a work on contemporary writers. As usual, he came running, ready and able. In one quick glance, he registered the essence of my art. He asked for my resume and drafted a text I really liked. He insisted on beginning with my training under Pierre-André Farcy, the conservator of the museum in Grenoble; he was an innovator, creating special rooms for modern art just after WWI. Boisdeffre then described the romantic watercolors from my period in Germany.

He added that I sought and found my own way to express my musings, in the style of Turner or Odilon Redon ! In concluding, he wrote: "Her rich and vibrant personality lends color and tone to everything Françoise Pène contemplates. For her, nature is not a theme of a school of painting but an invitation to happiness." I felt both fulfilled and anxious.

The date of the opening approached. I would miss the warm ambiance my daughters would have lent to the occasion, but I hoped my sons would attend because Pierre, afraid it would be tiring, had decided not to go.

Happily, one of Paul's cousins and a German woman – a former admirer of Didier – offered their help. Pretty girls with a current flair, they brought a nice touch to the opening which went as well as could be.

Television was represented by Adam Saunier who hosted a weekly broadcast every Sunday. He seemed very sure of himself and the segment he did on me was fast and missed the mark at the same time. He portrayed me as a novice painter – even though I had been going to museums and training at the museum of Grenoble since the age of thirteen. My friends who saw the broadcast were dumbfounded!

By contrast, the interview I did on the radio was a success. After a brief synopsis of my training, the interviewer had me discuss my development as a painter and my actual method of successive glazings, leaving a margin of uncertainty on the subject thus allowing the viewer to substitute his own reveries in place of my musings.

After three weeks of exhibition, I brought the unsold paintings home. Some acquaintances who wanted a reduced price came by.

The variety of my work allowed all these very different people to find something with which they were happy.

Following only my own impulses in my work, I appreciated critiques, especially when they were not just glowing platitudes. Pierre had his favorites and, though we lived together, still showed surprise at the quantity and quality of my paintings. Clo, too, and her favorite was my most admired piece. The assessment of the writer Christine Arnothy corresponded closely to my own self-criticism, causing her husband, Claude Bellanger, a Resistance comrade of Pierre and director of the newspaper "Parisien Libéré", to remark that, despite our age difference, we were kindred spirits. I was flattered.

With the nervous tension passed, I felt both satisfied and down. Daily life resumed, ever and ever more calm.

Clotilde moved from Paris to the house in Cier. After considering living together, the boys changed their minds. Olivier was preparing as fast as possible to marry a young woman from the Ardennes, a student at Fontenay, who was preparing for her "agrégation" competition in mathematics to become a teacher. He was twenty-three, she twenty-two when, at the beginning of the summer of 1966, Nicole, a tall, blond girl, seemingly sweet and determined, joined the Pène family.

The date of the marriage approached. At the preference of the interested parties, it was a lay ceremony and the lunch that followed took place at the "Palais des Princes" at the edge of the Bois de Boulogne near our home. On the wedding day, the couple was much admired. Olivier, in navy blue, looked younger than his years and Nicole, hair twisted into a chignon adorned with two small roses at the base, dressed in a white silk outfit, was dazzling. Rarely have I seen a young girl looking so pure and virginal on her wedding day. Nobody would guess that adorable Cédric was growing inside her slender body ...

Appearing recovered from his heart attack, Pierre resumed his full roster of duties for the Ministry of Public Works. In addition to inspections in the southern half of France, he prepared reports following each trip, attended numerous meetings with his colleagues, and established a rating system for the chief engineers, each defending his subordinates.

He also participated, under the friendly direction of Henri Michel, in the History Committee, specializing in the corps of Roads and Bridges during the Occupation. He was passionate about this research which gave him access to secret archives, sometimes discovering with disappointment the corrupt behavior of certain friends during that period.

Pierre was always intransigent with regard to those who helped Vichy and the Nazis ruin and dishonor France and also for having created racial discrimination. The reading of a weighty, confidential file concerning a former comrade we had first met in Madagascar and who was the chief engineer who furnished the most material and personnel to the occupiers, caused us to cease all relations with him.

Always very punctual, Pierre was nervously waiting for me to drive to one of his meetings when the phone rang. It was a friend of Florence, passing through Paris, bringing news from Boston for me. I managed to politely disengage. Crossing the garden to the Boulevard Anatole France, we heard a crash. The back of my parked "Daf" car had just been rammed by a runaway car. A few seconds sooner, having baskets to place in the trunk, I would have been crushed. And Pierre, who would have already been seated in the car, would have suffered a terrible jolt. Death did not want us, but was only temporarily put off.

We were spending the summer with Florence, Pete and their American children in Monaco, resuming a more luxurious lifestyle. We lunched at the Sea Club, a good seaside restaurant that was part of the hôtel de Paris; famous worldwide, it would later be destroyed and replaced by a modern structure, losing its Monacan character. Pat and Christine, Annette's daughters, came to join us before returning to Arras, their father Paul Guillaut's new garrison.

The entire seaside area, undeveloped when we first purchased our apartment, was in the process of a construction boom of tall buildings. Plans changed constantly, not only as a result of the caprices of the Prince but also those of Onassis, the rich and powerful shipping magnate, who owned the majority of shares in the "Société des Bains de Mer", that is to say the casinos, luxury beaches and the Hôtel de Paris.

With autumn approaching, we were thinking of our return to Paris but first we were going to celebrate my sixty-second birthday on September 17th at a new Chinese restaurant. Pierre even had the patience to accompany me to the good houses of couture to buy a dress for me. I chose a mustard yellow one in good quality wool.

In Boulogne, our sons resumed the charming tradition of having Sunday dinner with us. Nicole was always in a good mood. We would soon have a reunion with my sister-in-law because Pierre had to do an inspection in Toulouse, about sixty miles from their ancestral village.

Arriving in Toulouse, we bought cakes and clothing for our poor thirteen year old grandson, Gilles, who lived in a home for handicapped children, Les Marroniers, ten miles from town. A comely young woman welcomed us in and showed us to a class to see Gilles. He grabbed one of the toys, an accordion, and crouched on a bookshelf. Did he recognize us? Nothing would prove so. The other students cried out joyfully and began unwrapping the other packages.

"Kiss your grandma", the school mistress told Gilles. He hesitated, then obeyed, sweet, lost, more handsome than the other children. But his eyes were void of expression.

After congratulating the new supervisor –who admitted being a bit traumatized by her job– on her courage, we left in the direction of Cier, depressed, brought low by the mystery of these children marked for life: tragedy for them, tragedy for their family. They didn't seem unhappy, surrounded by devoted care, living in a group, and free. Gilles, who loved escapades, could even climb trees.

In Boulogne, where he was doted on by his mother and sisters, he had escaped via the balcony, jumping two stories, without staircase or railing, to a terrace, trying to get away from speech lessons Annette had arranged with a neighbor.

At Cier, we were kindly received by Clo who had us admire the transformations made to this old country house by a bit of work and the installation of Clo's furnishings from Paris.

Pierre then left for an inspection trip to Bordeaux and I took the chance to go to Arras, where Annette and Paul waited for me and my cargo of paintings to decorate their official army housing.

This austere town is dotted with beautiful monuments and a famous plaza that retained the homogeneity of its Middle Ages style. Annette and Paul's house was on the outskirts and banal. Each of my paintings found its place. I rearranged some furniture, convinced Annette to order a marble top for a coffee table, and we both picked out material for curtains. The Colonel and his wife could now receive their guests, the interior of the house now having more character than the exterior.

Following these two short trips, life in Boulogne had resumed its rhythm when a letter arrived from Clotilde, brutally and belatedly announcing the tragedy that had unfolded at Les Marroniers – the death of Gilles, and Annette and Paul's arrival after the burial.

It was an astonishing, mysterious message, without detail, stupe-fying. Thankfully, Pierre had just left again for Bordeaux and his absence would give me the chance to prepare him for this awful news.

Shattered, Annette and Paul were preoccupied at the moment with shielding from trouble the director of the home and the charming young woman who had greeted us, who was on duty in the infirmary when the incident happened. Little by little, I began to piece together what had happened. Gilles had had whooping cough and was in the infirmary on the fourth floor. During the evening, a caregiver had brought in a boy who had a serious cut. While the young girl tended to the newcomer, our sneaky Gilles took the opportunity to open the window, wanting to climb on scaffolding he had been playing on that day. Perhaps he wanted to avoid getting a needle or, as usual, was just fooling around.

Unfortunately, the scaffolding had been removed at the end of the day by the painters who had completed their work. Gilles didn't notice and tumbled into the void. When the nurse rushed to the yard, the child, already dead, was smiling at the notion of his escapade.

Knowing the difficulty of keeping their son from his escapades, Annette gave a statement to the police exonerating the staff. There was no question of allowing accusations against people who accepted responsibility to care for these poor children or to see closed an establishment as well maintained as "Les Marroniers".

Literally collapsing on learning of Gilles' death upon his return from Bordeaux, Pierre cried for hours. Thus I realized his vulnerability and the profound attachment he had for this innocent, bewildered, wild and touching child.

I was also grieving and profoundly depressed but it was Annette who suffered most. She alone had borne entirely the heavy burden of this child. It would take several years for her to accept this heartbreak.

The inevitable and monotonous condolences, which confirmed our deep feelings of Gilles' deliverance, always brought us back to the same question; had we done enough for him during his brief life?

When Cédric was born a few weeks after Gilles' death, Pierre composed a poem:

Le rameau étiolé, négligé par la sève,
végétait lentement, condamné à vie brève.
Tous les soins étaient vains. Mère, parents, amis,
tous étaient impuissants et mortels les soucis.

Un orage soudain, imprévu et brutal,
frappe la pauvre branche dans un élan fatal.
L'infortuné rameau projeté jusqu'à terre,
y tomba d'un seul coup, s'y brisa comme verre,
laissant le souvenir d'un ange silencieux,
hier encore réprouvé, aujourd'hui bienheureux.

Mais sur le tronc meurtri, un bourgeon verdoyant
pointe encore minuscule et déjà chatoyant,
promettant l'avenir, l'oubli de la disgrâce,
une vie accomplie, dans la joie et la grâce.

Pierre Pène, December 1966

*The wilting branch, neglected by the sap, grew slowly,
condemned to a brief life. All care was in vain. Mother,
kin and friends were all powerless to prevent his demise.
A sudden storm, unforeseen and brutal, broke the poor
branch, sending it in one fell swoop to the ground where
it shattered like glass, leaving only the memory of this
silent angel, yesterday troubled but, today, blessed.
But on the deadly tree trunk a verdant bud already
blooms, still minuscule but already shimmering, and
promising the future, the distancing of misfortune, and
an accomplished life of joy and blessings.*

Despite little Cédric's charm, we were concerned about this increase in responsibility on his parents. Nicole had to compete in the "agrégation" to become a teacher and Olivier seemed overwhelmed by the maternal tasks he had taken on to lessen his wife's load. Happily, Mme Dulin, Nicole's mother, came to live with them for a while at Massy; her husband, who couldn't stand being cooped up in an apartment, returned to his beloved Ardennes to tend his garden.

Florence and Pete came for a stay in Paris and Annette, alerted, came to see her sister. They went together to see one of their mother's paintings displayed at the Museum of Modern Art and rejoiced on learning that I was also selected for an exhibition in Cannes.

Our happiness at being surrounded by our four children, rare because Florence had married an American, brought back everyone's strength. I threw myself more and more into painting and also went to all the Parisian exhibitions.

After a marvelous show of Vermeer and his associates, an exhibition of Bonnard followed. His work, pleasing and intimate, consoled me for being figurative and not a follower of trends. The latter seemed easy to me compared to the works of Picasso, admired by thousands of visitors. Picasso was huge, adroit, imaginative, a braggart, a mocker, fiery-tempered ... I liked certain of Dali's works but he suffers lapses in taste, isn't sincere in his eccentricity, is too much of a publicity hound and is, above all, interested in money. He had the opportunity for a huge exhibition which attracted a lot of young people to the Beaubourg Cultural Center, launched by President Pompidou. Thanks to the planning, aggressive ugliness and publicity, crowds flocked to this pseudo oil refinery and modern art became popular.

Having attained the top ranks of the corps of Roads and Bridges, Pierre prepared to take a late retirement at seventy years of age, whereas chief engineers retired at sixty-five. He promised me a Mediterranean cruise and a trip to Israel.

He wanted at all cost to stick it out to the end despite his heart attack but, suddenly, as he was about to take his well-deserved rest, he started to feel poorly. Stupidly, I thought it was a reaction to the retirement because the symptoms appeared at the same time. I decided to take him for a few days to Clo's in Cier, his childhood home. But Pierre wasn't interested in anything, didn't eat the meals his sister prepared, and stayed laid up in his room, crying, chagrined and depressed.

When we returned to Paris, we consulted several doctors. My husband was suffering from prostate cancer which had metastasized to the cerebellum. Hospitalized for tests, he fell into semi-consciousness. At the end of five days in the clinic and despite a hormonal treatment, "Tace", his condition worsened. What to do? Wait for things to go either way? Have surgery to remove a hypothetical tumor from his brain? The debate began among family members and the doctors.

But at the end of eight days, the Tace finally had an effect. Bit by bit, Pierre became lucid again. He confronted the night guard who had restrained him and demanded champagne. He had celebrated the same way when he left the hospital in Monaco.

Back at home, he resumed his reading in three languages and our existence got back, little by little, to normal, despite the number of medications, uncomfortable treatments, and frequent suffering. Very cooperative, talking about everything and maintaining his sense of humor, my patient was happy to frequently welcome visits not only from his children but also from his colleagues and friends. We were getting along perfectly and he, now impotent, no longer chased skirts.

I always made sure he did not learn of the gravity of his illness. This shocked Olivier who had a high estimation of his father's courage. But there are different kinds of courage ... Pierre himself distinguished between bravery in a group — which he had demonstrated at age nineteen during WWI battles — and, at forty two, individual bravery — necessary in the Resistance during WWII.

Anxious and with a vivid imagination, he would go through unnecessary hardship by learning the truth, whereas he did accept bodily suffering thinking it leads to recovery.

He never uttered the word cancer but, a few days before his death, said to me: "I must know the truth ... what did the doctors say?"

"Your current crisis is serious and could last a long time, maybe three months, but you'll come out of it like before."

He seemed reassured, prepared to suffer but not to die.

Forewarned, Florence hurried to her father's bedside. It was a great joy for him but also a sorrow when she left. He noted it in his diary, which ends with that entry. The handwriting, still firm, softened and sloped downward for this sad entry. He probably knew he would never see her again.

During the last ten days of his life, Pierre could no longer drink or eat and the pain became intolerable. Widespread cancer being irreversible, the doctor announced he was going to stop the perfusions. My husband had a happy smile at the idea of no longer having to endure them while I suffered inside knowing the end was near.

On April 19, 1972, when Annette came as she did each evening to give, as the nurse did each morning, a shot of morphine to her father, Pierre was breathing shallowly. He said to me in a whisper "Come quickly, lie next to me".

The morphine took effect and he went to eternal sleep, peacefully, without pain, his hand in mine, cradled by my caress of his face.

The funeral was simple because I was literally exhausted by the months of caregiving, passed practically without sleep. I was so demoralized at finding myself alone after forty-eight years of life together exchanging ideas. My only consolation was that he was no longer suffering.

Annette, Florence and Nicole, realizing my despondency, gave me Patricia, Daniel and Cédric for a stay in Monaco. That obliged me to take care of myself and develop new living habits. But the nights are long because I am an insomniac. I have a hard time hiding the desire to die myself. Not to rejoin Pierre because I don't believe in an afterlife, but because my life is behind me and I am no longer indispensable to anyone.

It was by consensus that we decided that big family gatherings would become the exception rather than the rule. The couples preferred to have Sundays to themselves. Didier had his sports or his girlfriend on the weekend. And Florence was in Boston.

Little by little, I got used to this solitude, taking simple meals, quickly prepared and eaten at the counter of my miniscule kitchen, listening to the news of the world.

Portrait of Pierre Pène by Françoise, his wife

ELEVEN

THE FINAL YEARS

Well after Pierre's death, Gilles Perrault, a renowned author whose talent I had notably admired in his 1967 book, "The Red Orchestra", requested a telephone interview. He was undertaking a work on the OCM (Organisation Civile et Militaire), one of the major movements of the Resistance, and wanted to interview me as a widow of one of its member directors.

The historian, Arthur Calmette, having already written an exhaustive book on the group, I was reticent at first, but Gilles Perrault ultimately convinced me to help him out. He claimed to be writing a very different book capturing the tenor of the period for the families of the Resistance fighters, which he himself was too young to recall firsthand.

Our interactions were pleasant and I willingly answered his questions. I even lent him, without hesitation, documents likely to be of interest since neither Pierre nor I had been made to give anything away to the Nazis despite our arrests, Pierre's torture and the threats to our children.

I awaited the publication of "La Longue Traque" (The Long Hunt) expecting to find in it Pierre as he was: courageous, organized, prudent, subtle and proud of having succeeded in clandestinely fighting against a despicable enemy aided and abetted by the collaborating petainists, French fascists, and let's not forget those who denounced Jews, communists, freemasons and Resistance fighters for money.

Thus upon publication I began reading Gilles Perrault's work with great curiosity. It was nicely dedicated and I was happy to see it began with a synopsis of the author's career as a writer. But the rest profoundly shocked me.

For five years, Gilles Perrault collected documents and eyewitness accounts from survivors, seeming to laud the courage of these elders who had put themselves in danger. But he had concealed from us that he was a communist and a former lawyer specializing in lost causes. His objective in reality was to try to whitewash and rehabilitate the reputation of Roland Farjon, the indisputable traitor responsible for numerous arrests.

He derided the "ghetto of the XVIth arrondissement" insisting on the fact, by the way exact, that the original directors of the OCM were drawn, through friendship and affinity, from the ranks of wealthy families. But he forgot to say that the organization grew on the basis of commonly held ideals, regardless of social status, welcoming equally road workers or public works agents; they were often the best operatives in the network. In the Aisnes, for example, they were under the orders of three of the four chief engineers for the department. The orders were, of course, not to take on new members lightly, without proper vetting. This turned out to be an ineffective precaution. The traitor, the son of a senator, a rich industrialist from the north, was in fact Pierre's chief within OCM, trusted precisely because of his status, one of the first to engage in betrayal. Gilles Perrault continued his tale, unmasking actions that had remained secret until then, perverting them and insinuating their protagonists were naive and boastful. Pierre, who had suffered the most, after the Farjon family itself, from his betrayal by his friend and partner in escape, was made out to be ruthless.

* * *

In "The Long Hunt", we were not the only ones transformed into "careless and boastful idiots". The whole OCM was sullied. Our painful past was thus given over to jealousy from all quarters – collaborators, Vichy members, cowards. Why this maligning? To minimize the guilt of one man who caused so many arrests and deportations? To ridicule a fine apolitical movement like the Resistance on the order or instigation of the Communist Party with which the author appeared to be associated? How did Gilles Perrault dare, after having gratefully received our testimonies and recollections, to make irony and contortion of that which we had confided, amassing inaccuracies, particularly about the escape?

Certain major errors were particularly abject. Gilles Perrault mocked Pierre for thinking he was the instigator of the escape while finding it natural that Farjon pulled out a file with which to loosen the bars. Why should Pierre have been surprised at that when, in a package of foodstuffs I had had delivered to him via the translator Robert, (who probably himself sensed the impending Nazi defeat), I had secreted a penknife in a loaf of bread ! Monique Farjon had likewise had a package delivered. It was very probable she had slipped him a file.

If Farjon and Pierre's escape had been a set-up, why had the Germans, furious, rushed to arrest members of their families?

The interpreter, Robert, had informed us after the Liberation that the German, Schott, in charge of the OCM file, had placed those who had not talked under pressure in the same cell as Farjon. Why was he so violently angry at the escape of both a big catch and a turncoat? According to Robert, the unfortunate man who preceded Pierre in Farjon's cell, Jacques-Henri Simon, had been deported and died during the trip.

That Pierre officially testified against Roland Farjon, in all sincerity but reluctantly, came about for several reasons. When, in August of 1944, Pierre and I met clandestinely in the apartment of a friend, Pierre Turbil, I told him about my interrogation at Fresnes and what I had learned about Farjon. A while later, it was corroborated by the testimony of other Farjon victims such as his own brother-in-law, Lepercq, one of the OCM leaders who was incarcerated at Fresnes at the same time I was. He had revealed to Pierre, crestfallen and miserable, that he was not the only one to have been denounced by a friend.

Pierre realized that his comrades might suspect duplicity between himself and Farjon since they had escaped together. Pierre had no doubt of Farjon's guilt, first because Farjon himself had confessed, during their imprisonment at Senlis: "I turned you in". Obsessed with the idea of escape, having already tried in vain to do so, Pierre didn't think for an instant that he was being manipulated. On the contrary, he was sure he had instigated his companion to escape and that Farjon was seduced to do so because the Normandy invasion had already begun.

Despite the urgings of the victims, my husband was torn between two duties: support the one who, despite his betrayals, had helped him escape and find his first safe haven, or bring comfort to the families of the dead with an official deposition about Farjon's crimes. Contrary to what Gilles Perrault implies, Pierre was not motivated by a personal grudge. If Roland Farjon had given names under torture, our compassion and forgiveness would have been forthcoming. But things are never that simple...

Farjon had taken on responsibilities that Pierre and I thought were over his head. Despite the continued oversight of his secretary, Sofka Nossovitch (who was deported to Ravensbrück and liberated by the Allies) and of Princess Vera Obolensky (nicknamed Vicky in the Resistance and arrested and executed in Berlin), he took many careless risks before being arrested.

It appears he gave in after two painful weeks in the hands of the SS; the skillful Schott took charge of him, flattering him and holding out the promise of survival if he cooperated in the struggle against the common enemy, Russia. Used to the easy life, attractive and wealthy, and more dazzling than intelligent, Farjon let himself be seduced; not being fully conscious at first of the ramifications of what he was doing, he gave up his best friend, who was shot, and many others who were deported.

It was clear that we pitied Farjon and his courageous, naive and charming wife, but what could we do? The proof of his guilt was mounting and we couldn't fail to testify. We couldn't be sure if his suicide was true or false. He had admitted his guilt and was going to be tried and probably would have been released after two or three years, cleansed of so many serious failings, since he was related to de Gaulle and his father was a member of the upper class.

Our family and friends were all shocked and distraught by the evil maligning Gilles Perrault had committed against a true Resistance fighter; his inventions, mistakes, and twisting of facts ridiculed the real heroes for the purpose of whitewashing the culpability of the real guilty party.

Perhaps certain members of the Resistance had exaggerated their accomplishments but at least they had all managed to hold up under pressure and not give up a single comrade. Farjon had betrayed some fifty people. As Didier so rightly put it, even if he had given up just one it would have sufficed to accuse him of treason.

Happily, Pierre had been dead for many years and would not seethe in anger reading "The Long Hunt". Relating this story which played such an important role in our lives, I myself am very troubled. A dialogue between Gilles Perrault and me went nowhere. Didier, very supportive of me since his father's death, penned an exquisite letter worthy of a highly educated professor which made more of an impression on the writer than my raging, slapdash missives; I was mortified at my misplaced trust.

Many other events would punctuate my life before its end. Some would be tests, such as Florence's divorce; she landed well on her feet and met Harry Levin, a passionate and idealistic man devoted to the third world. Other events would be happier, such as the marriages of my grandchildren and the births of great-grandchildren.

On the artistic front, I veered into creating collages which elicited many compliments although I didn't make much effort, probably out of laziness or lack of ambition, to get them exhibited.

In writing this memoir, I have sought above all else to cover a time gone by, animating the family and its life by describing our problems and those of our contemporaries. It is a memoir of our family, a guide that will perhaps help my descendants, to give direction to their lives, to familiarize them with their roots, and with the ethics with which Pierre and I led our lives.

He was brilliant and interesting but, as his mother warned me on the day of our engagement, temperamental and vulnerable. He wanted to appear perfect and I played along. Had I succeeded?

Having no particular religious conviction and not believing in afterlife, I, on the other hand, am profoundly certain that each person's life continues through his descendants. Ours being already well established, I can only feel secure and, satisfied, end this story. I am united, with all my heart, with the destiny of my descendants.

P.S. The wait for the final departure is almost over. Three times I have been close to death:

First, in Ethiopia, where my heart failed due to malaria. I pushed back the sheets, passive, until I thought of my two daughters who would have a stepmother. That rallied me.

In the dungeon at Fresnes in 1944 when I collapsed from weakness and malnutrition. The guard saved me with hot soup I was unauthorized to receive because I had opened my window.

In Baden, following a ping pong party, my heart failed. I had double bronchial pneumonia. The newly developed penicillin saved me.

Death, I await you, but please don't make me suffer too much.

Françoise died shortly after turning ninety-three. She knew it that very morning and alerted us via the nurse. We were all with her when she passed away, without fear or suffering, peaceful and courageous.

9 781931 475679